Character
COUNTS

BRINGING THE ROTARY
FOUR-WAY TEST TO LIFE

ISBN: 9780982798133

CORINNE A. GREGORY

Character Counts: Bringing the Rotary Four-Way Test to Life

Published by Maestrowerks, LLC.

Printed in the United States of America

Gregory, Corinne A.

"Character Counts: Bringing the Rotary Four-Way Test to Life"

Cover Design and Layout by Dawn Teagarden

Edited by Richard Jarman

ISBN: 978-0-9827981-3-3

Warning: Disclaimer
The purpose of this book is to educate and entertain. The author or publisher does not guarantee that anyone following the techniques, suggestions, tips, ideas, or strategies will become successful. The author and publisher shall have neither liability nor responsibility to anyone with respect to any loss or damage cause, or alleged to be caused, directly or indirectly by the information contained in this book. This is a fully independent work by the author. Rotary International has not participated or endorsed this work in any way.

*To my husband, Patrick Sharpe — Thanks for
being such a huge supporter, for your boundless
encouragement and undying belief in my work.*

*To Sarah Spaeth — Believe it or not, you are the reason
this book has become reality. Sharing an adult beverage at
Alchemy and telling you about this book that was "stuck"
inside me turned out to be the spark that lit the flame.*

—ıιι—

*And, lovingly, to Wenonah Finch Sharpe — you who have
written and edited so much, individually and together
with Grant...I am honored that you were "impressed" that
I'd written a book. We miss you, Nonie....it was an honor
to be your daughter even if it was for such a short time.*

ACKNOWLEDGEMENTS

The process of "birthing" this book has been a long one, and there have been many people who have been involved in this journey—some knowingly, others not. I'd like to take a moment to give them credit for their roles in making this happen.

First, to Helen Ralph. She was my sponsor at my first Rotary Club—Woodinville Rotary (I still think of you guys as "home," by the way). Helen was so welcoming and so gracious as she led me around during my first meeting, it left a lasting impression. Helen is now at the North Kitsap/Kingston Rotary and was present when I received my member's badge at East Jefferson Rotary (Chimacum, WA).

To John Matthews (PDG 5030, Mercer Island Rotary, WA and soon part of Rotary International) I just have to say "THANK YOU" for all the inspiration and support I have received from you over the years. Your positive feedback about my presentations and enthusiasm for the SocialSmarts program paved the way for my having the courage to write *this* book. Speaking at District Conference on your recommendation remains one of my Rotary highlights.

Several Rotarians and members of the Rotary "family" have assisted in varying ways in support of this book. Cherry Jarvis, Amy Howard, Michael Locander, Alan Marsh, Erv DeSmet, Chris Boland—you all gave me great input on the early scripts and content for the crowdfunding campaign and more. The breadth of your perspectives helped me fine-tune it and certainly made it much better than it would have been without your feedback! I was fortunate to have some amazing reviewers for the book early on. Susan Ness, Petra Walker, Gerald Sieberhagen, Ray Serebrin, Chuck Udell, Hal Stevens—you all added so much with your comments and insights. I can't tell you how much I appreciate your taking the time to read what I put down and thoughtfully send suggestions for improvement.

I personally "blame" Jack Butcher of Federal Way Rotary, WA for being the straw that broke the camel's back. Jack contacted me back in June of 2016, asking if I'd consider speaking to his club based on things he read on my blog about the Four-Way Test and my viewpoints on Rotary. On August 11, 2016, I officially announced this book with the knowledge that once I said it was coming, there was no going back. Thanks, Jack, for your amazing faith in me and the value of my writing.

To those who are such active participants in commenting on my newsletter content—you have stimulated so much thought and, as you'll see, many of your comments and suggestions made their way into the book. I send a thank you to Marty Lindeman, Dr. Bob Steinberg, Jeff Cornish, Michael Scharmett, Darwin Husa, Norm Noble and many more. I value the dialog with you all and look forward to much more!

Richard Jarman—again, you did an awesome job on the edits. You have this gift of tweaking things just so, and I love working with you. Dawn Teagarden, you, too, are a great addition to the team. I love what you come up with for design and look-and-feel and you are a joy to work with.

Finally, I have to take a moment to thank the many financial backers of this project. I started a crowdfunding campaign to help underwrite some of the costs of book production and I am indebted to each and every one of you who participated. Some of the largest contributors included my in-law Sharpe family members Christopher, Kathryn and Loretta, my mother Eva Neumann, daughter Alana Fiske, long-time Rotarian friend Howard Gutknecht, another long-time supporter Ben Reppond, client and friend Tony Magee, my "virtual sister" Wendy Sawyer. Other Rotarians who graciously participated include Jack Butcher, Gerald Porter, Darwin Husa, Ray Serebrin, Meredith Wagner, Cherry Jarvis, Larry Howland, Ina Agafonova. Support from other friends such as Jeff Sanders, Brian Kelly and Max Painter was hugely appreciated—in some cases, we haven't known each other for too long, but your belief in me means more than I can say!

Not only are your individual donations and contributions invaluable to the success of this book, but collectively you have made this campaign evergreen: funds are still needed and appreciated as the book is published and I begin marketing. If you want to make a contribution, go to CharacterCountsRotary.com and you'll be directed to the crowdfunding page.

If I've missed anyone else, I sincerely apologize. It's not meant to be personal—there were so many people involved in so many ways, it's impossible to thank you all here. This is as much your book as it is mine.

October 26, 2017
Port Ludlow, WA

CONTENTS

INTRODUCTION

May I be direct? Among the greatest literary works or speeches written, none are shorter than this. We are talking about a mere 24 words—two dozen. Today, they guide 1.2 million individuals across the globe. There is no way to know how many Rotarians have recited this motto in the over 112 years since the first Rotary meeting was convened in Chicago, Ilinois. At that time, the Rotary Four-Way Test didn't even exist, but it has become the perfect pledge for an organization formed to foster fellowship and service. The Four-Way Test is intended to be used to evaluate whether a thought, word or action is in keeping with the Rotary spirit, and the organization's objectives.

The purpose of this book is to take a detailed look at the Four-Way Test: examine how it came to be, what the components mean individually and *in toto*. I also offer a number of case studies and stories of Rotarians who have lived the concepts of the Four-Way Test. It's my fervent hope that this book is a useful guide to current Rotarians. But more than that, I hope it can become a resource to share the mission, purpose and significance of Rotary to prospective Rotarians, including our youth.

I have been blessed and honored to be a Rotarian for many years, but I believe my own "career" in Rotary is still in its infancy. There's so much about this organization, and the members that bring it to life. I hope to offer more as I learn more.

Before I dive into the book, I'd like to give you a little background about how it came to be. The "birthing process" of "Character Counts: Bringing the Rotary Four-Way Test to Life" is just about complete. But like a child springing from the womb, I'm hoping this "baby" is only just beginning to see life.

The Six-Year Itch

The earliest timestamp for the outline of this book reads 2011. I kid you not. This book is SIX YEARS in the making. No, I haven't been writing it for six years. But I came up with the concept that long ago. Now, here it is, 2017, and it's just about done. Crazy...

But, it's a reflection of my own life. It's been rather tumultuous over the past several years and my writing has suffered. In 2010, I had just written and released my first self-published book, "It's Not Who You Know, It's How You Treat Them." I was speaking nationally and internationally, sharing my presentation "Overcoming Failure to Educate." This presentation tied the long-standing deficiencies in our children's education to the lack of teaching of social skills and character. Many of my presentations were to Rotary Clubs, because my SocialSmarts' curriculum included the first question and elements of the Four-Way Test.

As part of my presentation, I had mapped the four questions of the Test to their underlying character foundations. When I first created that slide, I felt a shiver of excitement come over me. Although I'd been a Rotarian for years, I didn't realize that what the Four-Way Test represented was a test of *character*. And, as I thought more deeply about what the questions were saying, I realized that each one of them had a slightly different perspective on what character traits were embodied.

It was eye-opening for me to think about the Four-Way Test in that way, and I was excited to see the reaction I got from Rotarians when I gave my speech. I gave that presentation for years, all throughout my own District 5030, then beyond. Rotarians commented on how they'd never thought of the Four-Way Test — and education — in this way.

Then, in February 2010, Rotarian Magazine did a feature article on me and my SocialSmarts program. The article was entitled "Talking Etiquette with Corinne Gregory." Suddenly, the speaking requests came fast and furious, from all parts of the county. I was asked to give speeches to youth at RYLA. I had "virtual" meetings with Rotarians across the nation to discuss SocialSmarts. Rotary Clubs offered to sponsor the curriculum in local schools. I was overjoyed to see how Rotary could use my program to introduce our organization and its beliefs to young students.

Every time I traveled, I contacted a Rotary club local to where I would be and offered to be a speaker. Kansas, Georgia, the greater Washington DC area, California, Oregon, Grand Cayman and more. In the Bahamas, my Rotary contact arranged for a meeting of all the area club Presidents, for whom I did a special presentation, and then later shared with the membership of East Nassau Rotary. I was speaking so often, I jokingly said I was on the "Rotary diet" because sometimes I'd be having two, or even all three, meals a day hosted by different clubs.

My book, "It's Not Who You Know, It's How You Treat Them," was my initial effort to bring the SocialSmarts program to the adult and professional world. It, too, contained references to Rotary and the Four-Way Test as a result of posts I'd written in my blog. It was great being able to share this book with Rotarians I met in the clubs I presented to.

In late 2010, then-District Governor John Matthews was at one of my presentations and we had a chance to chat afterwards. He said the message that I was sharing really resonated with him and what he had come to observe at Costco, where he was Senior Vice President. John thought I should share my message more broadly. Imagine my surprise when I was invited to give an extended version of my presentation at the District Conference in Portland! It was my first time at a Rotary Conference, and the exposure to so many talented and dedicated individuals was life-changing.

The presentation was quite successful. There was great feedback from both sessions I offered, and it led to more regional appearances. After one particularly memorable meeting at an international club, several of the members invited me out for a glass of wine afterwards. One member asked if I'd ever considered presenting at the International Conference and when I said I hadn't, she insisted I should, and she would help make some connections.

That's when I got scared. Local and regional presentations were one thing, but who was I to think I had a message that would be of interest and value to thousands of Rotarians from all across the world? I would be presenting in front of people who had been intimately involved in Rotary before I was even born! I had already started on the Character Counts book, having drafted about half of Chapter 2, but the fear of building on my local success stopped me in my tracks. I was terrified that I would put out a book that would not be worthy of the tremendous reputation and success of Rotary, and the many members who made it what it is.

Fast-forward three years. I'm sitting in a local wine bar, chatting with two friends about my writing experience. We get on a topic of the books I want to write. I explain I've been on a pretty dry streak of late. I tell Sarah about the Character Counts book idea. I realize I'm talking about it with passion and conviction, like it already existed. I tell her, "well, this book has been stuck inside me for years," and she tells me I *have* to write it.

While I agree with her, once again I set the idea aside. Frankly, I'm still afraid that the book will not be worthy—I don't want to fail. I don't want to fail Rotary and I don't want to disappoint current and future Rotarians with something I've put into permanence.

Finally, in July of 2016, I am on a trip, helping my husband deliver a yacht up to Alaska. I decide to revisit "Character Counts." I look at Chapter 2 again, and make some notes. I examine the working title and realize I hate it. In a flash of inspiration, I come up with the idea of "Bringing the Rotary Four-Way Test *to Life*" and realize, "that's it!"

At the same time, I get an invitation from Jack Butcher of Federal Way Rotary to come speak at a meeting. He has been spearheading a movement within his club to get back to Rotary's "roots." He tells me that some of the best stuff he's read about what Rotary means is from my own blog. I am honored and deeply humbled.

So, cut to the chase: I accept the invitation and realize, if I'm ever going to get this book done, I'd better start with the visualization. I get together with my book designer and she creates a great cover. With the visual in hand, I craft my presentation for Federal Way Rotary and include the announcement of the new book.

On August 11, 2016, I share the message and the pre-announcement with Federal Way Rotary. It's been nearly five years since I've presented at a Rotary meeting and I'm nervous, particularly because the club is having it videotaped. It wasn't my best performance, I'll admit, but I finally did it: I told the "world" I was writing the book, and so I needed to do it to remain accountable.

Why this Book? Why now?

I don't think anyone will argue that we live in very divisive times. Whether you follow the daily arguments and rages in the political arena, or are concerned about racial and ethnic tensions, or ponder the religious and cultural differences in the world, it's clear that we find ourselves in a very tumultuous place. The question of ethics—both personal and professional—has never been more topical than it is now.

Technology and other factors have led to a younger generation that is generally more concerned with themselves than with the needs and wants of others. It's difficult to get our young people (and even many adults) to take their eyes off a screen and fingers off a keyboard and connect with people in the physical world. People who are disconnected from each other often see "truth" as relative, and make their own rules based on what's right for them.

But, Rotary bucks that trend. Rotary's precepts are built on *inclusion* at a time where there is so much divisiveness and strife in the world. Every day, across the globe, Rotarians meet for fellowship and service. We are connected by common beliefs and a common mission. I've had the tremendous experience of being welcomed as family, regardless of which club I'm visiting. The experience of being a Rotarian, of believing in and practicing the Four-Way Test, and sharing Service Above Self is a unifier, comforting and inspiring in a climate of dissension and mistrust.

Format and Conventions Used

A couple of quick notes about the book. Each chapter begins with a quote, intended to set the tone for the chapter. Generally, the quote is from a Rotarian, but there are a few exceptions. At the conclusion of the chapter discussion, I have tried to summarize the main points, both as a recap and a way to condense the detailed content.

Finally, I end the chapter with a section I call "Your Turn" in which I offer some points for consideration, and pose some questions to spark discussion or thought. Sometimes the questions may be a bit challenging, but I want to explore varying aspects of a character trait or point. You may want to share these with your own Rotary club or another group you are involved in. I would welcome any feedback you may have as a result. Please do let me know if I can share your comments broadly!

You may also see that I use specific capitalization conventions in the content. When I'm discussing a particular character trait or concept, I will capitalize the word. For example, to illustrate the concept Integrity, I use a leading capital. This is to differentiate the concept itself from ordinary prose.

Final Thoughts Before We Begin

The process of writing this book has been an amazing experience. I've had to research like I've never done before. I've met people, both in real life and virtually, that have humbled and inspired me. What I have learned and what I'm trying to share in these pages has given me goosebumps at times. I still worry that it may not be worthy,—I received one scathing comment early on that almost made me quit writing—but I realize if I don't write it, I'll never know. While I ask myself "what if it fails?" I am almost as intimidated by the thought, "well, what if it succeeds?"

When you put yourself out and try to create something educational for others, it's natural to think that you may not get everything right and not everyone will agree with you. I'm by no means an "expert" in Rotary. My expertise lies in social skills and character, in how to treat others with respect and be ethical in dealings with others. I share what I know, and what I believe. It's not "gospel," but I hope it's informative and thought-provoking. I offer you the best I can do, and I pray it is a worthy work.

I will continue to offer updates and content through my blog. Feel free to visit or even subscribe. You can find relevant posts about Rotary here: http://corinnegregory.com/blog/category/rotary/

Thanks in advance for picking up this book. I hope you find it of value and that it either offers you something new or reminds you of something you already knew but may have forgotten. I welcome your thoughts and feedback. You can reach me at corinne@corinnegregory.com

CHAPTER 1

A BRIEF HISTORY OF ROTARY AND THE FOUR-WAY TEST

*"I knew if I could get them to think
right, they would do right."*

— *Herbert J. Taylor*

The year is 1932. The United States is in the midst of the Great Depression. Unemployment stands at a record 24%. Joblessness in Germany, Australia, the UK and Canada is even worse. Widespread bank failures prompt citizens to withdraw their money, preferring to keep their funds in cash or gold. This exacerbates the economic crises stemming from the stock market collapse in 1929, and the lingering financial stresses brought on by World War I.

Shanty towns, or "Hoovervilles" as they are known in the US, spring up all across the country. They are built with cardboard, scrap metal and wood, or anything that can be used for shelter. Severe drought and over-farming causes the Midwest to experience catastrophic dust storms. The result is farm failures, loss of livestock and loss of human lives. Franklin Delano Roosevelt is elected President in November. The country is hopeful he will be able to turn the tide of hopelessness and financial adversity.

In the midst of this chaos, Herbert J. Taylor sits in his office, head in his hands. He is agonizing over what he can do to reverse the imminent bankruptcy his company, Club Aluminum, is facing. "Business as usual" isn't working. Taylor knows something must change. What was about to happen changed not only the future of the company—it literally changed the world.

ROTARY—THE EARLY DAYS

Much has been written about how Rotary began, and how it has grown to be one of the largest service organizations in the world. For those unfamiliar with its history, I'd like to offer a brief bit of background.

In February of 1905, attorney Paul P. Harris convened what would be the first Rotary meeting with three other business acquaintances: Gustave Loehr, an engineer, Silvester Schiele, a tailor, and Hiram E. Shorey, a coal merchant. The original meeting took place in Loehr's Chicago office, but the plan was to rotate meetings among each others' offices—hence the name "Rotary." But, the first club expanded so quickly that it outgrew the rotational office plan. Instead, they adopted the practice of holding regular weekly meetings at a set location. Paul Harris would be the first Rotary Club President, serving from 1910-1912.

Rotary Clubs quickly sprouted up in cities along the West Coast. San Francisco, Oakland, Los Angeles, and Seattle were early adopters. In 1910, the National Association of Rotary was formed. In 1911 Rotary grew beyond its US boundaries when a club in Winnipeg, Manitoba, Canada was born, followed soon after by a club in Dublin, Ireland. As a result, the name of the organization was changed to The International Association of Rotary.

Soon after, more international clubs sprung up in London, the Philippines, Cuba and India. By 1922, the Association changed names again, this time becoming Rotary International. By 1925, there were over 200 clubs in existence around the world, with over 20,000 members.

The mission of Rotary International is to bring together business, professional and community leaders in order to provide service to others, promote integrity, and advance world understanding, goodwill, and peace. As such, Rotary is focused on six specific areas of emphasis:

- Promoting peace
- Fighting disease
- Providing clean water, sanitation, and hygiene
- Saving mothers and children
- Supporting education
- Growing local economies

Today, Rotary International supports over 1.2 million members in more than 35,000 clubs across the globe. Members come from all walks of life, cultures, languages, experiences and interests. The one common denominator is that they come together for fellowship to promote service. But, this didn't happen overnight, and we still have a way to go to learn how the Four-Way Test came to be the motto it is today.

Herbert Taylor's Epiphany

Herbert J. Taylor, the aluminum executive with the failing business, was in trouble. His company, Club Aluminum, was bankrupt. A new line of cookware was experiencing dropping sales. Taylor felt that, while other measures needed to be taken to increase the company's profitability, the underlying need was to find some practical ethical yardstick or motto for his employees to use when interacting with customers, suppliers and the public.

Taylor tried to come up with a motto based on several guiding principles he believed in. As a devout Christian, he couldn't find exactly what he was looking for (we'll learn more about the inspiration for the Four-Way Test in Chapter 9). His initial drafts were considerably longer. At one point, he had a 100-word draft and a Seven-Way Test. Finally, after more thought and prayer, Taylor wrote the Four-Way Test on a small white piece of paper, and it appeared as we know it today:

> Is it the TRUTH? Is it FAIR to all concerned? Will it build GOODWILL and BETTER FRIENDSHIPS? Is it BENEFICIAL to all concerned?

After a period of personal testing by Taylor, and a review period by several company managers, the Four-Way Test was adopted by Club Aluminum. Taylor even had the phrase copyrighted. Within five years of implementing the Four-Way Test, not only was Club Aluminum no longer in bankruptcy, but the company was highly profitable, able to issue a million dollars in dividends to its stockholders, in spite of the continuing Depression.

Taylor was a Rotarian at the time he wrote the Four-Way Test, having joined Rotary in the 1920s, but the Test was not intended to be a Rotary slogan. Taylor himself worked hard to promote the Four-Way Test within Club Aluminum and beyond, through radio broadcasts, speaking opportunities and work with various youth groups. In 1939, he became President of the Rotary Club of Chicago and even became District Governor and a Vice President of Rotary International in 1945. Rotary Director Richard Vernor, asked Taylor in 1942 for permission for Rotary to use the Four-Way Test.

By the time Taylor became the President of Rotary International in 1954, the Four-Way Test was being used in Rotary clubs all around the world. To commemorate Rotary's 50th anniversary, Herbert J. Taylor was featured on the cover of *Newsweek*. Despite his Rotary connections, Taylor established the "4 Way Test Association," a non-profit independent from Rotary to help promote the Four-Way Test outside of Rotary's organizational structure. Currently, Allen Mathis III, Herbert Taylor's grandson, is the president of the association.

The Four-Way Test remains the ethical guide for Rotarians in their professional and personal lives. It has been translated into over 100 languages and is regularly recited at Rotary meetings and functions. Clubs around the world conduct "Four-Way Test Speech Contests" and "Four-Way Test Essays" for children and youth. There are Ethics in Business Awards given to professionals who conduct themselves with the highest of standards. Some are specifically for Rotarians, but many recognize business and community leaders regardless of their Rotarian affiliation.

In the 112 years since Rotary was founded, its accomplishments worldwide, are nothing short of astounding. Whether bringing fresh water to an underdeveloped third-world village, providing dictionaries to third grade students, or eradicating the global polio epidemic, Rotarians create positive change in the in the world through cooperation, service and support. And, regardless of whether you attend a meeting in the Philippines, enjoy Rotarian fellowship at an event in South Africa or India, or attend a District Conference or even Rotary International Conference in cities across the globe, you are part of a huge, global family where the members are all guided by the same 24 words.

SUMMARY

- This chapter provided a short history of the man who penned the Four-Way Test, Herbert J. Taylor and how the Test came to be. As the head of failing Club Aluminum, Taylor felt he needed to come up with some "ethical yardstick" that was easy for his employees to remember to guide their conduct both internally and externally.

- At the time Taylor wrote the Four-Way Test, the country—even the world—was in the middle of the Great Depression. In spite of the economic challenges, five years after implementing the Four-Way Test as part of the company's operational philosophy, Club Aluminum was no longer failing, and had issued significant dividends to its shareholders.

- Even though Taylor had been a Rotarian for many years when he wrote the Four-Way Test, it was not then intended to be a Rotary slogan. Taylor promoted the Four-Way Test through his own efforts for years, before being asked in the 1940s to allow Rotary to adopt. By the mid-1950s, the Four-Way Test had been fully integrated into Rotary International and remains one of the most recognizable mottos representing Rotary.

- Taylor went on to form the "4-Way Test Association" to provide for a way to promote the Test outside of

Rotary. It's now run by Taylor's grandson, but has no Rotary affiliation.

- While the Test consists of only 24 words, it would be hard to find another set of precepts that can-say so much, with so few syllables. Across the globe, Rotarians from all walks of life, circumstance, cultures and interests are all guided by these words to serve the world and do good, for the sake of humanity and the world we live in.

YOUR TURN

In this short introduction to the Rotary Four-Way Test, we looked at the history and significance of the 24 words adopted by Rotary International to promote ethics. While in subsequent chapters, I'll offer more and differing prompts for discussion and thought, this chapter lends itself to just a few.

- ❏ If you were to rewrite the Four-Way Test, given what you know about today's world, would you change it and, if so, how?

- ❏ Is there anything you feel is missing from the Four-Way Test?

- ❏ Does your club or District have some sort of "Four-Way Test" contest or award to actively promote the concept and practice of the Four-Way Test to the public? If not, what could you do to share this important motto with your community.

- ❏ Does your club recite the Four-Way Test? Why or why not?

CHAPTER 2

QUESTION 1: IS IT THE TRUTH?

"If you tell the truth, you don't have to remember anything."
— *Mark Twain*

The first question in the Four Way Test is very basic. It reminds us to determine whether the intended interaction is truthful and real. Unless we begin by answering this basic, foundational question, it's virtually impossible to proceed. Think about it: if you aren't sure whether someone is being truthful, where can your interaction go? How can you build a fruitful relationship?

Certainly, there are people who lie, cheat and steal their way through the business landscape. But I don't consider you "successful" if your "success" comes at the cost of lost integrity. I'd rather be poor, yet able to look myself in the mirror and like what I see, than be the richest person in the world, knowing that I got there by being ruthless and dishonest.

In this chapter, we'll examine the basic character foundations of Question 1—Honesty and Integrity. We will see why something as simple as basic truth is critical to productive dialog and relationship-building.

HONESTY

honesty (n)
a: fairness and straightforwardness of conduct;
b: adherence to the facts

There's a great line in a Billy Joel song that really sums up what we too often see in the world these days:

> "'Honesty' is such a lonely word,
> Everyone is so untrue..."

This certainly applies to the business world. But you can find a lack of real honesty anywhere. In many ways, we are becoming a nation—a culture—of liars. Truth is a rare commodity these days. Just consider how much we now rely on lawyers, courts and "special committees" to determine and enforce "the truth" because people lie, sneak around, cover up, and renege on commitments and contracts.

In his book, *Tangled Webs: How False Statements Are Undermining America,* author James B. Stewart examines high-profile perjury cases. He shows that they not only undermine our judicial system, they in some ways unravel the very fabric of our society. Mr. Stewart talks about several "celebrity" cases such as the Bernie Madoff fiasco, Barry Bonds' lying about steroid use, Martha Stewart's insider trading debacle and others, making the point that celebs who perjure themselves are rarely held accountable, even though people know they are lying. It seems that, if they are really good liars, they get away with their misdeeds.

This doesn't just happen in celeb cases. It also happens in everyday life. Truth is not valued the way it used to be. I have personally seen egregious cases of documented, written perjury, where the lies were spelled out in clear text. Yet, in spite of all the contradictions, and even lies told on the stand, no one was held accountable.

The downstream ramifications of this lack of truthfulness are huge. Our kids are learning that the 11th commandment is "Don't Get Caught." They don't believe lying or cheating is a big deal. Recent studies show more than ⅔rds of high school students have cheated on a test. We have difficulty trusting or believing others because we know that people will tell us anything just to make inroads, to get out of trouble, or to make themselves into more than they really are.

When we talk about truth, we know that many will argue that truth is subjective—that everyone has their own truth. We won't argue that point here. When we talk about truth, we are especially concerned with determining whether what someone says is factual and accurate. It's true that everyone has their own opinions. One person might tell you that this restaurant has the best Mexican food in town, while another says it's the place across town. But they are being honest about their opinions, and accurate in what they are saying. That is what we specifically mean by "truth."

The Whole Truth

Another definition of honesty involves being truthful without being misleading. It is tempting to embellish the truth at times. We are generally ego-centric creatures who want to feel important and valued. That can result in additions or omissions to the truth, from the fisherman who tells the story of "the big one that got away" (that gets bigger with each retelling of the tale!), all the way to pretending that the fancy corner office really is yours when it's not. Although no one else may know the difference, we do. Being truthful to oneself is as important as being honest with others. And, frequently we find it challenging to be truthful with others because we are unable or unwilling to be honest with ourselves.

Let's examine some of the reasons why we are less-than-truthful at times. Those reasons include:

- Fear of negative consequences if we admit to what really occurred
- Fear of what others might think of us if we tell the truth
- We haven't done — or don't want to do — something that we should do, or have committed to do
- We're covering up for another untruth we've already told

If you think about it, it's our own basic insecurity that keeps us from being honest. But the ramifications of not being truthful go beyond just us. When we fail to tell others the whole truth, we're showing a lack of respect for the other person. Sometimes we use the excuse that we are saving someone's feelings by fibbing or being less-than-honest, but my philosophy has always been "I'd rather take a bad truth than a good lie." Even if the truth is hard to accept, when someone is being honest with you, you know where they stand.

Dealing with people honestly is a core requirement to building and maintaining relationships. Telling the truth may be difficult at times, but it's easier than fabricating stories or omitting facts. If the real truth comes out, and you are found to have been dishonest, your future credibility is suspect . You've potentially risked damage to relationships, positions, and reputations.

INTEGRITY

integrity (n)
firm adherence to a code of especially moral or
artistic values

It seems that every few days, you hear some story about violations of ethics and integrity. It could be insider trading, a company being awarded a contract under preferential circumstances, or "kick backs" being passed on to a lawmaker in exchange for a vote. Lack of integrity is all around us.

Integrity is one thing you cannot buy, although it appears lately that many try. Integrity is a complex and multifaceted character trait. This is part of the reason we will be revisiting it later, after we've looked at more of the individual character components of The Four-Way Test.

Simply put, Integrity is the essential core of character that says you can be trusted to stand by your word, your principles, and your beliefs. It also means that you know the difference between right and wrong, and put that knowledge into practice.

Because of the importance of integrity to having good moral character, the two concepts and phrases are frequently used interchangeably. That's not just mere convenience, either. When you have integrity, of course you keep to your principles, as I said previously. However, not only are you true in your treatment of and conduct to others, but you are true to *yourself*. So, your actual character is embodied in the concept of integrity.

The challenge with integrity is that it's an all-or-nothing proposition. Integrity means doing the right thing *no matter what*. The way we explain it to our SocialSmarts® students is that your character is who you are and what you do, no matter *what else you are doing*. You stick to your principles even at the potential "cost" of your own personal gain. Let me give you an example:

A dear friend of mine was involved with a high-tech company for some time. As a result, he was offered a good number of stock options as his compensation. The more my friend became knowledgeable about the company, the less he agreed with the way they did business. When he left the company, rather than cash in, or even retain the stock options for future exercise, he returned them to the company. As he explained to the head of the company, if he kept the options, he would remain connected to the company through those options, and, frankly, because of their differences in beliefs, principles and way of doing business, he wanted nothing further to do with the company. It cost him quite a bit of money. But he would rather remain true to his principles than to have the money.

Million-Dollar Integrity

Here's another example that many of us would find hard to follow. Let me ask you: is your integrity worth a million dollars? It was to Brian Davis in the Spring of 2010. His actions are what should earn him a place in the history books for exhibiting positive character.

On an April weekend in 2010, Davis, a professional golfer on the PGA tour, was playing against Jim Furyk in the playoffs at the Verizon Heritage tournament. Davis was just about poised to win his first-ever PGA tournament, when a shot he was taking out of some weeds went awry. He ended up hitting a stray weed in his backswing...a mistake that would cost him two penalty strokes, if he were caught. A weed...not likely anyone would see his club hit something so small, even on high-definition television.

But, Davis saw it. And he called the penalty *on himself*. He admitted to the errant swing, with the net result that Davis conceded the game to Jim Furyk. Furyk went home with just over $1M in prize money.

If it were you, and a million bucks was on the line, would YOU have pointed out that penalty? It's probably easy for us all to say, "Sure!" but would we REALLY have?

This episode in golf is an illustration for what we all should learn: character and values are in play all the time, no matter what we are doing and who is around. It's like the saying, "If a tree falls in the woods and no one is there to hear, does it make a sound?" We should be true to the person we are, anytime, anywhere, even if no one is looking. Our soul, our character, our conscience should be worth at least a million dollars because once our reputation and honor is gone, it is hugely difficult to redeem.

Another word often used to mean the same thing as Integrity is "honor." Honor means "following the rules for doing the right thing." It also refers to one's good name or public esteem—in other words, your reputation. Being known as a person of integrity means you have a stellar reputation; your word is your bond and you can be trusted. When someone else can put that much faith in who you are and how you conduct yourself, there can be no higher praise. Integrity is that important.

However, today, the "new integrity" has come to mean something quite different. If you look at the business leaders and lawmakers who have all taken a fall because of their lapses of character, you quickly see that the "new integrity" means being very, very sorry for doing wrong once they were caught. But, no longer is it the guidepost that keeps them from doing wrong in the first place.

While they may say all the right things and look contrite on camera as they face their shameful behavior in public, you wonder how real the remorse is. Have they learned the lesson that it's wrong to *do wrong*, or have they just decided to be more careful not to get caught in the future? We can't say for certain, of course, but it is an important lesson — integrity is a fragile thing. Once broken, it's hard to restore. The greater the lapse, the more visible the cracks, even after you've faced your consequences.

Honor Is Fragile

One way we illustrate this "Honor is Fragile" concept in the SocialSmarts® curriculum (*Exploring the Virtues II for Upper Primary Grades*) is by using the following exercise on "Vanishing Integrity." We start by arranging three glasses where the class can easily see them. The first two glasses contain plain water, which will be used to represent the two participants in the story we have the instructor share with the students. The third glass is half full with ordinary household bleach.

> "Ryan and Trevor are two <insert grade level or age of your students here> boys that have been friends for a long time. Most of the time, Ryan tries to do the right thing, like obeying his parents, but for some reason, Trevor seems to always be getting into trouble. For example, Ryan leaves the house in the morning and gets right to the bus on time, but Trevor is forever goofing off and frequently misses the bus. Trevor also likes to be kind of a bully and throw rocks at the neighborhood cats.

Well, one morning before school, Trevor was pitching rocks at the cats and accidentally hit a neighbor's window, breaking the glass. Trevor got scared and quickly ran to the bus stop, got on the bus and never told anyone about the broken window."

As story progresses, the instructor (or a designated student participant) adds one drop of dark food coloring to "Trevor's" glass each time they come to an incident of his wrongdoing. The instructor mentions that, at the beginning, when Trevor only does one thing wrong, you really can't see the water change color. But, with each new drop, the water becomes more and more "stained" as the repeated wrong-doing starts to affect Trevor's character and his whole "person" (represented by the glass). Ryan's glass, in the meantime, remains clear because he is trying hard to always do the right thing.

As the exercise progresses, we explain that as Trevor's water becomes darker, he is also becoming more miserable. His friends are tired of hanging out with the troublemaker because they are afraid they'll get in trouble, too. They stop spending time with him. He himself is getting tired of repeatedly getting detention or losing privileges, and he's starting to feel very trapped by the lies he has to tell to get out of more trouble (like the broken window). Finally, after he has a serious talking-to by the school principal, Trevor decides he has to do something about all this trouble. He starts by going to the neighbor whose window he broke, admits what he did, and offers to make good on the broken window by paying for its replacement.

During this part of the story, the instructor takes a little of the bleach from the third glass and adds it to "Trevor's" glass each time he does something to make good on his wrongdoing The instructor shares things Trevor can do to "repent" like being more honest, apologizing to his friends for getting them into trouble, etc. The students will notice that with each little "penance," Trevor's water gets a little clearer until it's almost totally clear.

At this point we ask the students about what they think would have happened if Trevor would have started changing his ways after only one or two drops of coloring had been added to his glass (Answer: it would have been easier and quicker to clear up his "stain" because the longer you wait to clear up lies or other acts of wrongdoing, the harder you have to work to recover, until it's almost impossible to get back to a "clear" conscience.)

We also ask the students about the difference between Trevor's and Ryan's glasses (Trevor's will still have a little color left in it). We use this to draw a parallel between the color of their glasses and the effects of wrongdoing on our lives. Finally, we mention that when you always try to act with honor and integrity, you avoid getting "stains" on your character. As a final wrap on the exercise, we share the quote "When you base your life on good principles, 99% of your decisions are already made." (Author unknown)

While "Vanishing Integrity" may seem like a pretty simple exercise, it's very powerful for communicating the value and fragility of Integrity. As "Trevor's" water gets more stained, we ask students whether they would be willing to take a drink out of that increasingly-murky glass. Even after the integrity has been "restored" with the bleach solution, most students *still* wouldn't be comfortable drinking out of the previously-stained glass. It's as though they are still skeptical of the quality of the water, even though it appears to be clean again. The valuable lesson is this: it's hard to rebuild your integrity, once it's been compromised.

Talking about Trustworthiness

TRUSTWORTHINESS

trustworthy (adj)
worthy of confidence, dependable

Remember the Aesop fable of the Boy Who Cried Wolf? The shepherd boy, seeking attention and excitement, falsely alarms the villagers that a wolf is threatening the grazing flock. Repeatedly, the shepherd boy calls the villagers up the mountainside to help protect the flock; each time the villagers discovers that there was no wolf. Finally, when a wolf actually appears, the villagers, weary of the many false alarms, refuses to charge up the hillside again. The shepherd boy could do nothing but watch in helpless horror as the wolf killed the sheep.

Being Trustworthy is practically synonymous with being dependable. "Dependable" is defined as being "capable of being trusted." It means that people can trust that you will do what you say you will do or do what you are expected to do. In the fable above the villagers depended on the shepherd boy, but lost their faith in the boy to the point where, when an actual emergency came, no one from the village responded. His dishonesty was the flock's—and his—undoing.

Promises and commitments
Part of being Trustworthy involves having other people know that they can put faith in your promises and commitments. Being known as someone who can be trusted and depended on is crucial to business and personal success. People value the comfort of knowing that what you say is believable—that what

you agree to do will get done. When people know they can put their trust in you, they can relax around you because they know that you respect and care about their feelings and needs.

When making promises and commitments, be careful about using the words "never" or "always." These absolutes imply a permanence that you may not be able to keep, due to unrealistic expectations or unforeseen circumstances. If you make repeated unrealistic promises, this again can erode people's confidence in your ability to keep your word. Make "good" promises—those that are realistic, achievable and within your power—and keep them. That's the surest way to build credibility and trust, two essential building blocks for developing and building positive relationships and influence.

SUMMARY

- The essential character components supporting the First Question in Rotary: Is it the TRUTH? are Integrity, Honesty, and Dependabilty.

- All over the world, the value and practice of truthfulness is eroding. But honesty with people is necessary if we intend to build and develop positive relationships. While there are many reasons people choose to be less-than-honest, they don't justify the dishonesty. In the end, they simply chose to be dishonest.

- Integrity means you will stick to a predictable high standard of moral conduct, no matter what. There are times you will be tempted to violate principles of decent behavior. Violating our integrity hurts us. And, once you have tainted your integrity, it is very difficult to restore it.

- Integrity is an essential piece of our character. People of integrity can be inherently trusted. You can depend that they will act in a way that is consistent with their character. They keep their promises. The art of making good promises—ones that are reasonable, achievable and within a person's power to complete—is an important part of building trust and dependability.

YOUR TURN

A concept is only useful if you put it into practice. In this section I offer a few ideas to consider when assessing your own conduct in light of the First Question of the Rotary Four-Way Test. These are only meant to be suggestions, not absolutes. Feel free to be creative with these as you wish!

❑ Consider your own tendency to "stretch the truth" or to tell "little white lies." Sometimes we may be slightly less-than-truthful to someone, for example, in order to spare someone else's feelings. Can you think of a way to respond truthfully, yet still preserves your original intent?

❑ On the flip side, when striving to be truthful, be aware of how "truthful" you can be and still be kind. If someone asks you what they think of a work assignment they have submitted, rather than being completely negative, think of a positive comment you can make. For example, "I see you are on the right track but I think you could use a little more research on point X" is much kinder—and more effective—than saying, "This is a waste of my time reading this. It's not even close to finished." Remember, for every negative, there is likely to be one or more positives.

❑ How good is your record of making and keeping promises? If it could be better, think about where you are getting tripped up. Do you make too many commitments because you want people to like you? Do you feel pressured to step up when others won't? Over-commitment is one of the biggest obstacles to completion. Maybe you make promises that aren't reasonable or achievable—setting yourself up to fail. Worst of all, do you make promises with no intention of keeping them because you think it won't matter, or that someone else save you? Making promises you can't—or won't—keep puts pressure on you and everyone around you, and hurts your credibility.

❑ There's a verse in the New Testament of the Bible that says "Let your yes be yes and your no be no." It's a great idea, regardless of your religious leanings. Let people trust that you mean what you say, and that you say what you mean. People appreciate when they know you are truthful with them. Practice honesty all the time, and the strength of your conviction will impress.

CHAPTER 3

QUESTION 2: IS IT FAIR TO ALL CONCERNED?

"What we have to do...is to find a way to celebrate our diversity and debate our differences without fracturing our communities."

— Hilary Rodham Clinton (Honorary Rotarian)

The second question in the Four-Way test is intended to determine the fairness of a situation. We all strive for fairness in all our dealings in life. We want what we believe we deserve. Of course, others feel the same way about their own needs and desires. In business and in life, we generally place a great deal of importance on whether or not we are being treated equitably.

Many of the problems and conflicts we see in our communities and, frankly, in the world come from people who feel that they are not being treated fairly. While Fairness and Equality are values we strive for, it's important to understand that those terms don't mean the same thing to everyone, and fairness may not always lead to an intended result. In this chapter, we will explore these character traits in greater detail, and see some of the impact they have had on Rotary—and the world.

FAIRNESS

fair (adj)
a: marked by impartiality and honesty: free from self-interest; b: conforming to established rules

"It's NOT FAIR!" We've all heard it, usually from a five- or six-year old who is having a tantrum when they have been denied something they want, or something someone else got instead of them. While we may instantly think of a child's response to an event, the reality is that feeling slighted when something doesn't go our way is a reaction we really don't outgrow. We may learn to respond better to perceived or actual unfair treatment, but it doesn't mean we like it any more as adults than we did as kids.

Fairness is very important to establishing trust. Being fair requires that you adopt a more outwardly-focused approach, one that takes the needs of others into consideration. This is more difficult than it might appear at first. Remember that we are born as intrinsically "me-centric" creatures. A baby doesn't stop to consider whether it's a convenient time for others to stop and change its diapers. It will cry for attention and expect to be accommodated. It's all about "my needs NOW."

As we get older, most of us learn to adjust our needs and wants around the wants and needs of others. It's part of maturing and it's crucial to positive relationships. But there is still that basic underlying "Me first" instinct that gets triggered when we feel we are getting an unfair deal.

Of course, some people never seem to outgrow the need to come out on top, no matter what. You can usually spot them a mile away. Their favorite word is "I." In any situation, they are looking for what they can gain, how they can negotiate the best deal for themselves, without regard for the other person. When dealing with these kinds of people, there is no easy trust. Instead, interactions with them are loaded with red flags and caution. Even when they seem to be "giving" you something you think is fairly due you, you can't help but think, "What are they really after? What am I missing?"

In today's culture, fairness can be very hard to come by. The overriding ideologies seem to be "get as much as you can" and "look out for #1." But that mentality is counter-productive because, when you are only looking out for your self-interest, others become equally competitive and protective of *their* own interests.

If you use Question 2 in assessing your interactions with people, you will find that being fair requires you to compromise sometimes. In some cases, being "fair" means putting aside our own wants and desires because of the needs or wants of another person or group. Often, If you are able to compromise, you may discover that the other party is willing to do the same thing. When you adopt this practice as a regular way of conducting yourself, you build trust. People come to know you as a person who can be depended on to be fair. This is a very important part of building relationships and keeping them strong. When you treat others fairly, the likelihood increases that they will treat you with fairness as well. The paradox is that "giving in" on your position initially sets you up for a better outcome, and leads to greater satisfaction for both parties.

Fairness, by definition, means finding an equitable balance of positions. It also implies conforming to a standard set of generally-accepted rules. Sometimes being fair requires assessing the rules when they, by their very nature, don't provide for a an equitable position. In the next section, we'll take a look at what we mean by the second part of "Fair"—that position of Equality. How does it relate to Question 2? We will find that the very foundations of Rotary had to change in order to conform to its own Four-Way Test.

EQUALITY

equality (n)
a: the quality and state of being equal: the quality or state of having the same rights, power, social status, etc.

equal (n)
1: of the same measure, quantity, amount, or number as another [equivalent]
2: regarding or affecting all objects in the same way [impartial]

As we saw in the previous section, the very notion of Fairness means that there is a sense of balance or evenness in an interaction or negotiation. The idea is that the parties involved give each other equal consideration for their wants, needs and position. We see in the definition of Equality that we are talking about "having the same rights, power, social status, etc." When you don't have this balance, someone is going to be the "loser" in the situation. That can lead to hard feelings, anger—or worse.

Countries go to war, with hundreds of thousands of people uprooted or killed, because of conflicts that cannot be solved equitably.

Equality is a simple concept in theory. But it's very difficult in practice. And, what is considered "equal" and "fair" at one point, can change over time, as generally-accepted rules or conditions evolve. In that circumstance, what used to seem balanced, suddenly no longer seems fair.

Redefining "Equality"

We are certainly all familiar with the struggles of the Civil Rights movement in the United States in the 1950s and 1960s, where people of color demanded equal treatment in society and under the law. Ultimately, Fairness was at the core of the struggle: just because certain people were perceived as "different," it did not mean they were less-worthy or less-deserving of equitable treatment.

While the fight for African-American equality was a huge, defining moment for the United States, it wasn't the first time minorities had to struggle to be counted as equals. In the latter part of the 1800s, the rights of women to be counted as equals and to have a vote entered into the national dialog. Women across the country — and in many parts of the world — questioned how it could be fair that women were considered less valuable, intelligent or worthy than men.

One notable supporter of women's rights was Woodrow Wilson, the 28th President of the United States. The two-term President, a member of the Rotary Club of Birmingham, Alabama, was a big believer in "global democracy" and tirelessly pursued the ideas of fairness and compromise. A strong advocate for the equality of women, he endorsed the 19th Amendment, giving women the right to vote.

Incidentally, on another front involving Fairness, Wilson was also instrumental in establishing the League of Nations, an intergovernmental organization founded as a result of the Paris Peace Conference that ended the conflict in World War I. The primary goal of the League was to settle international disputes through negotiation and arbitration—tools for keeping things fair and equitable,—as well as providing for just treatment of native peoples, protection of minorities, policing human and drug trafficking, overseeing fair and humane treatment of prisoners of war, and monitoring the arms trade. For his efforts in sponsoring the League of Nations, President Wilson was awarded the Nobel Peace Prize in 1919.

But, just because Wilson helped ensure women were granted the right to vote did not mean that they were automatically "equal" in the eyes of society and the world. Even our very own Rotary International, with its membership blossoming across the globe, lagged behind when it came to offering women a place at the table.

During the same period that the US was in the middle of the civil rights' conflict, Rotary itself was in the midst of a redefinition of what its membership was all about. In the 1950s, a Rotary Club in India proposed the idea of removing the word "male" from the Standard Rotary Constitution. In 1964, a proposal by a Club in Ceylon (Sri Lanka, now) to allow women to be admitted was voted down by delegates of the Council of Legislation. Two other proposals asking for permission to admit women were also withdrawn. In 1972, a Club in the US brought a proposal asking for permission to admit women to the Council of Legislation. At the 1977 Rotary International Convention, three more proposals were presented to the Council and one Brazilian club suggested allowing women to be admitted as Honorary Rotarians, but not as full members.

While the process to officially admit women to Rotary dragged on, the Rotary Club of Duarte, California took matters in its own hands and allowed women to join. This was in violation of the Standard Rotary Constitution—the move cost the club its membership in Rotary International. The club filed a lawsuit in the California Superior Court, challenging Rotary International's gender-based qualification for membership, but lost. While the California Court of Appeals reversed that decision, the fight continued to the US Supreme Court. During this same period, Rotary clubs in several countries, including India, the US, Sweden and Switzerland proposed that club bylaws and the Rotary Constitution remove references to its members as "male persons."

On May 4th, 1987, a ruling by the US Supreme Court removed the restriction of women as members. The Rotary Club of Marin Sunrise (California) became the first club to admit women as its charter members, and, as a just and fitting act indicative of the new era, the Rotary Club of Duarte, recently reinstated, elected Sylvia Whitlock as the first women club President. Then, finally, the 1989 Council on legislation voted to admit women to Rotary clubs worldwide.

By 1990, just a few short years after the Supreme Court victory, there were over 20,000 female Rotarians. Five years later, no less than eight women were elected district governors. In 2005, the first female trustee of the Rotary Foundation began her term, and in 2008, the first woman was elected to the Rotary

International Board of Directors. And, by 2013, Anne Matthews was the first women to be vice-president of Rotary International. Today, there are more than 200,000 female members of Rotary International and our numbers are increasing. It may have taken Rotary nearly 60 years to change its policies and practices, but today Rotarians of all genders can agree that this change was Fair to all concerned.

THE DIFFERENCE BETWEEN FAIRNESS AND EQUALITY

While the concepts of Fairness and Equality are certainly very similar and complementary—in reality and practice they are not the same.

Recall from the previous section that we defined Equal as "identical in value, magnitude, or some specified quality." In the applications we have been exploring in this chapter, that would mean both sides in a negotiation, for example, would get the exact same quantity or quality. But, that doesn't really happen all the time, does it? And, if it doesn't, does that mean a situation isn't fair? Let's look at that a bit more closely.

Before we go into the negotiation side of it, let's take a look at a very simple example, and see how equal doesn't necessarily mean fair. It's dinner time and we are about to sit down at the table. Among our diners are a 205 lb. male high school football player and a six-year-old petite little girl. Now, what do you think would happen if you dished up the equal amount of food for each of these two diners? Do you think it's realistic that the young girl is going to need—or even be able to eat—the same amount of food as the football player? She likely won't be able to eat half, right? What if you balanced it out the other way and served her normal portion to the high schooler? Is he going to be full or even satisfied on what the little girl typically eats? No, of course not. And, frankly, having the expectation that either diner is going to be happy with the same amount of foodas the other person receives isn't even realistic.

Fairness really means that everyone gets what he or she needs, not necessarily an equal amount. Fairness, even mathematically speaking, is a virtue of *differences* — making things right and even in the face of a real or perceived inequality. Equality is simply... sameness, as in 1+1=2. That is the only correct answer. Equality is simple. Fairness, being able to determine what is balanced and right in the face of an imbalance, isn't quite so easy.

Instead of a black-and-white, identical measure, what we are really striving for is *equity*. Being equitable, according to Merriam-Webster, implies "amounting to the same thing in worth or significance." So, in other words, balanced. By looking at the relative worth or significance of a thing, we can determine whether two sides (or three or four) are being treated fairly.

Essentially, Fairness is about providing evenness to each side, as far as is practical or feasible. Fairness implies that there is an impartiality or unbiased disposition. It's the characteristic of being just to everyone, treating them without favoritism, prejudice, or discrimination.

We all recognize that people are not created equal, and that, as a result, we cannot always treat people equally. Equal wouldn't always be fair! There are people who are born very smart, and others who are not as intelligent. There are those who are able-bodied and others who have disabilities. There are individuals who are rich and those who are not as well-off. Differences between gender, sexual orientation, religious and cultures all impact how we adjust circumstances to promote Fairness. What we are striving for is to treat people in an even-handed manner, with the same respect and consideration that is due anyone.

If we go back to the example of the little girl and the high school football player at the dinner table, Fairness means that they get a meal served to them that is appropriate to the amount of food they can eat. In education, we strive to level the playing field for students who have learning disabilities by providing them with extra resources or developing a personalized learning plan geared toward helping them be successful on a level they can achieve. In the job market, we accommodate workers with physical limitations or disabilities by creating workspaces that support their needs, such as wheelchair access or amplifying equipment for those with hearing issues. It may not be realistic or practical—or even fair!—to expect an amputee to lug a huge firehose as required by an able-bodied firefighter, but that does not mean the amputee doesn't have a place in the fire department if that is his or her dream.

But, while we may strive for Fairness and Equality in the world, we must also recognize that life isn't always fair. Bad things happen to good people and the hero doesn't always get the girl (or boy). Our obligation, as Rotarians, is to do the very best we can to ensure that our dealings with people are fair and just. As with many other actions, we can't control what other people do, but we can control what *we* do, and, hopefully, we can also serve as an example to others by our behavior.

As a final thought on Fairness, consider that the word itself has its origins in the old English word "faeger" which means beauty. Just imagine how beautiful the world would be if we all treated one other with fairness and committed ourselves to equity among all men and women.

SUMMARY

* This chapter found us diving deep into the character traits underlying the Second Question in The Four-Way Test: Is it FAIR to all concerned? The traits we defined and examined were Fairness and Equality.

* Fairness means that there is an impartiality and openness in our dealings with others. To be fair, you need to consider not just your own wants and needs, but those of others — their wants and needs are just as valid as yours. Many of the problems we see in our own communities and in the world stem from a belief, perceived or real, that something is not being handled fairly. Our minds are wired to expect fairness, and, it can be upsetting or anger-provoking when we feel we are not getting our due.

* Equality means having the same in quantity, value or status. In practice, it requires a balance because not everyone can have the same thing or be identical, therefore making things equal isn't always possible or practical.

* Because it's not always possible to be *equal*, the true test of Fairness is to ensure that things are equitable. In other words, keeping things in balance so that the quality of each side is preserved in a neutral, unbiased way. In this chapter we looked at some examples where fair didn't necessarily mean "equal," showing that the two concepts are shared and related, but are not always the same.

* Treating people fairly is a huge building block to developing and maintaining positive relationships, whether personal or professional. When others know

you will deal with them fairly, it works to create mutual respect. On the other hand, operating with an agenda of self-interest erodes trust and respect. When people know you are only looking out for yourself, they respond by being more guarded in their interactions and protective of their own needs. Being fair in your dealings with others is the quickest way to be sure others will be fair with you in return.

- But, as we know, life isn't always fair. There will be times where we do our best to be fair and just, and things just don't go the way we'd hoped. There will be circumstances beyond our control, and one of the biggest things beyond our control is the thoughts, actions and behaviors of others. We can merely do our best, do the right thing, control our own actions, and find the beauty in how we conducted ourselves.

YOUR TURN

Here are a couple of thoughts to explore when considering the underlying concepts of Fairness and Equality. Some of these may be easy. Others may be a bit more controversial. But this section is intended to stimulate thinking and discussion.

- ❑ Consider how many times you say (to yourself, or out loud) "That's not fair!" Examine the circumstances around your feelings. Is the situation itself not fair, or is someone causing the imbalance? What might be a better way to handle these circumstances?

- ❑ Some things seem "fair" or not depending on your own perspective, situation or belief. One example is taxation. Should people who earn more money pay the same rate in taxes as someone who earns less? Is a flat-tax a more fair way to assess taxes or is a variable rate more balanced? Should someone who is more affluent pay more into government programs to compensate for those who are financially disadvantaged?

- ❑ What about Fairness in the workplace? Do you see any examples of discrimination in your office or place of business? How are customers of varying types treated? Are there any employees receiving preferential treatment?

- ❑ Family life can be a huge area in which to explore Fairness. Are adults and children in the household being given equitable freedoms or privileges, or are some members of the household unfairly burdened with responsibilities or chores? How can things be made more fair?

❑ Gender equality is a big topic these days. Where, in your opinion, is the line between "fair" and "equal?" While it may be easy to agree that clubs such as Rotary should permit individuals from both genders to join, how far should we extend the concept of "gender neutrality?" Should we be allowed to dress the same, hold all the same jobs, use the same bathrooms? Where is the dividing line, or is there one?

CHAPTER 4

QUESTION 3: WILL IT BUILD GOODWILL AND BETTER FRIENDSHIPS?

*"Friendship...the craving for which brought
Rotary into existence is the thing that will keep
Rotary a living, vital force in the world for all time,
the very foundation of our organization."*

— Albert S. Adams (Rotarian, Rotary Club of Atlanta,
GA)

The third Question of The Four-Way Test requires the use of a complex series of character traits that must be used together to work correctly. The character traits we will be examining in this chapter are

* Empathy

* Caring & Compassion

* Kindness

* Respect

In addition to defining and discussing each of these traits separately, we'll also explore how they work together to address the requirements of Question 3.

While Question 3 specifically refers to "friendships," and, of course, developing friends is a vital part of our existence, the broader term might really be "relationships." Certainly, Question 3 is intended to be applied to all interactions, so it would be proper to assume that this important evaluation would be applicable in any relationship—professional or personal.

EMPATHY

empathy (n)
the action of understanding, being aware of, being sensitive to, and vicariously experiencing the feelings, thoughts, and experience of another of either the past or present without having the feelings, thoughts, and experience fully communicated in an objectively explicit manner

Empathy is a very significant emotion necessary for building and maintaining relationships. It means having the capacity to understand or feel what another person is experiencing, based on your own perspectives and experiences. It's what makes our stomach cringe when we think about a child skinning a knee on the asphalt. We know what it's like to be sad, lonely or in pain, so we can put ourselves in the place of anyone we encounter who is in need.

The origins of the word Empathy really help explain the meaning. The Ancient Greek word *empatheia* means "physical affection or passion." The Germans adapted the word to create *Einfühlung*, which literally translated is "feeling into." It is about seeing with someone else's eyes, or, as the saying goes, "walking a mile in someone else's shoes."

Generally speaking, we are born with empathy. Have you noticed that, when one baby in a nursery begins crying, they all start to fuss and cry? Of course, there are some notable exceptions — individuals who lack empathy due to some pathology, such as autism and other psychological and emotional disorders. As a rule, empathy is an innate trait. At the same time, if not properly nurtured and supported, empathy can be damaged or destroyed. Individuals who have experienced trauma or abuse, or were exposed to situations where others showed a lack of empathy towards them, frequently feel reduced empathy towards others themselves.

Empathy is an interesting concept, too, in light of the discussion in the previous chapter on Fairness. Studies have shown that high degrees of empathy lead to greater altruism in individuals. Altruism is defined as any behavior that benefits another person or group. Conversely, lower degrees of empathy make individuals tend toward greater egotism, or the pursuit of personal gain over that of others. An individual with greater empathy, then, would be someone for whom Fairness is important because they can relate to that need in others. Fairness would matter much less for someone with compromised empathy because for them, what others feel or think is relatively unimportant.

CARING & COMPASSION

caring (n)
the provision of what is necessary for the welfare and protection of someone or something, a sense of responsibility toward another

compassion (n)
sympathetic consciousness of others' distress together with a desire to alleviate it

Two other closely related virtues behind the sentiment of Question 3 are that of Caring and Compassion. In order to do what is being called for in Question 3, one has to *care* about others—how they think and feel. As the definition says, the welfare and protection of someone or something must be within your awareness. If others don't matter, then we are back to the egoistic "self," without regard to others around us.

Most people deeply desire to care about something and someone, just as they want someone to care for them. The reciprocity of this feeling and desire binds people together. Caring is a very broad term, that implies an interest and concern beyond oneself. But it's only a feeling—it does not contain action.

Also related to Caring, Empathy and Compassion are words that are often used interchangeably. They are, however, not quite the same thing. Empathy involves relating to the feeling someone else is experiencing. Compassion goes further, not only understanding that pain or plight, but also including the desire to do something to ease that pain or difficulty. Whereas

Empathy allows us to relate to people's emotions and conditions, Compassion is what compels us to respond when we hear someone cry, or find someone is cold and hungry. Compassion can be hugely compelling, motivating us to drop everything and respond when there is a need, regardless of personal impact or consequences.

Frank Borman (Rotary Club of Space Center, Houston, TX) is one individual who exhibited a great deal of compassion, and it spurred him to action. Many of us know Frank as the Apollo 8 astronaut who led NASA's first ever moon-orbiting mission in 1968. Prior to that, he was also the Commander of the Gemini 7 mission, which made the first rendezvous with orbiting spacecraft.

Though these events are enough to consider Frank a hero, it is a different act, years later, that define him as a Rotarian of note. After retiring from the space program, Frank joined Eastern Airlines in 1970 as one of its executives. On the evening of Friday, December 29th, 1972, Frank received a call at home. An Eastern Tristar Jumbo Jet had crashed in the Florida Everglades killing 101 people, out of a total of 176 people on board. While there were certainly many people and resources who were available to assist in the search and rescue after the crash, Frank himself rushed to the scene, jumping into the muddy swamps, assisting with the rescue of victims and loading survivors into waiting helicopters.

One account from a surviving passenger, Al Morris, stated that he found himself attended to by a man who jumped from a helicopter and sloshed his way over to where he was. The man took off his own coat, and put it around Al's shoulders. Al recognized his rescuer as none other than Frank Borman, recently made a vice-president of Eastern. Borman then proceeded to get him to the waiting helicopter. Frank's personal response to the Flight 401 tragedy is an exemplary act of compassion because he ignored all risk and potential danger to himself to help the victims and survivors of the crash.

KINDNESS

> **kindness (n)**
> 1: a kind deed
> 2: the quality or state of being kind

Kindness is fundamentally related to the other traits we have been discussing in this chapter. Kindness means being caring, compassionate, loving and considerate. A kind person not only shows concern for the feelings of others, they also tend to do good deeds without consideration of praise or reward. People who are kind tend to be helpful, generous and pleasant. It's no coincidence that people who are kind are also considered ethical because of their regard and right treatment of others.

Kindness is an outwardly focused virtue, directed toward other people. But being kind is also a vital way of bringing meaning to our own lives as well. Practicing kindness enables us to communicate better, be more compassionate and to be a positive force in people's lives.

There are many different facets of kindness. There are the obvious ones: being kind to others, and to yourself. But we don't automatically assign kindness to entities beyond those in human form. We can show kindness to:

- Animals
- Resources and
- The Environment

We also show kindness by being respectful and considerate of "other dwellers" in our world. This is also very important, and it impacts us directly and indirectly. When we visit a forest or beach, we take care to leave a minimal footprint and not disturb nature and its inhabitants. We practice recycling and composting because of the huge amount of garbage humankind generates every day. We also can be aware of waste in other areas—food, water, power—and recognize that there are people in other parts of the world who lack what we take for granted.

As our lives become busier and increasingly fractured, it's easy to overlook simple kindness. We see evidence of road rage, divisive language, rudeness and plain disregard for others everywhere we look. Yet, how difficult is it to stop and give a stranger the gift of a kind word or smile, to hold a door open, or offer a helping hand? Never underestimate the power of kindness: literally, lives have been saved by a kind word or deed at the right time. Kindness costs you nothing and yet can be priceless to the recipient.

RESPECT

respect (n)
a: a high or special regard, the quality or state of being esteemed

All of the character traits we have covered in this chapter really revolve around one over-arching concept: Respect. As we think about this basic idea of respect, I'm sure you would agree treating people as though they matter is highly important. Yet, respect is becoming an endangered species.

In my earlier book, "It's Not Who You Know, It's How You Treat Them," I noted a Gallup poll from 2002 which reported that 80%

of Americans thought lack of courtesy and respect was a serious national problem. Around the same time, an ABC News poll shared its conclusions that 73% of Americans thought manners and behavior were worse than 20-30 years ago. By 2006, ABC News reported that 84% of Americans "often saw" people "being rude and disrespectful." Take just 30 seconds to consider the amount of hatred and disrespect flung at political candidates of all party affiliations in this past election, as one example.

With so much disregard for other people's feelings, opinions and experiences, it's no wonder we are becoming used to being overlooked. Social media hasn't helped matters either: rudeness, incivility and outright cruelty to others is rampant in chat rooms and other gathering places on the Web.

Our youth, who are the most connected of any age group on the planet, are hugely vulnerable to this type of behavior. "Garbage in, garbage out" is the perfect metaphor for what our children are experiencing. They witness disrespectful behavior towards adults and authority figures in a "funny" cartoon like "Rug Rats" (ok, I'm dating myself a little here, but I found this show absolutely appalling when it first aired) or participating in an "online" environment like "After School" which provides the perfect "anonymous" vehicle for hate-speak and cyberbullying, to watching adults verbally crucify each other in nightly "news" programs...is it any wonder our kids lack respect, empathy and compassion for one another?

The basic idea of respect is not difficult: give other people the simple courtesy of being regarded at least as highly as you regard yourself. Respect does not mean you must be chummy, or even *like* each other. But you do need to treat them with civility and accept that they have a right to their own values, experiences

66

and opinions. While many people would say that respect needs to be earned, I would rather assume that everyone, by default, deserves to be treated with respect. If someone behaves in such a manner that you lose respect for their actions or integrity, you should still treat them with civility.

Due to the importance of Respect as the basis of the Four-Way Test, Rotarians have an excellent opportunity to impact the world by how they treat not only other Rotarians, but the world at large. In 2015, Rotary International President K.R. Ravindran shared in a speech to the Parliament of the World's Religions that

> "In Rotary, every religion is respected, every tradition is welcomed, and every conviction is honored, for in Rotary, we join in friendship and are bonded by our dedication to service."

That is the challenge and obligation Rotarians have in their dealings in the world. When you treat people as though they are equally deserving of the common good, everyone stands to benefit. As President Ravindran said, "Charity and serving those with the greatest needs...is what Rotary is all about."

One individual who took this calling to heart was the late Sir Edmund Hillary (Rotary Club of Auckland, NZ), the globally recognized mountaineer. He and his Nepalese Sherpa Tenzing Norgay, became the first confirmed mountaineers to have summited Mt. Everest in 1953. While we instantly recognize him for his feats of determination and bravery while tackling treacherous mountain peaks, it's what he did with his life after the ascent of Everest that I'd like to applaud him for in this chapter.

Hillary, as any mountaineer attempting ascents in the Himalayas will attest, learned to appreciate the support and partnership of local Sherpas. His appreciation and respect for the Sherpas led to his founding of the Himalayan Trust in 1960 to address the problems the Nepalese people faced. Hillary approached the Foundation's work by respecting the rights of the Sherpas to have input into what assistance they needed, rather than to just tell them what the Foundation was going to do. He said, "We always responded to the wishes of the local people." In conjunction with support from the Rotary Club of Mount Victoria (Wellington, NZ), the Trust has been able to build over 25 schools, has awarded over 100 scholarships annually to Nepalese and Sherpa students, built two hospitals and several more village clinics to provide health and medical care, constructed drinking water systems, and much more.

Hillary as philanthropist has left a legacy of essential services to people who would likely otherwise been overlooked. His compassion, respect and kindness towards the Sherpas and Nepalese was recognized by the nation in 2003 when they awarded Hillary honorary citizenship on the 50th anniversary of the summiting of Everest. His efforts and actions are consistent with the Third Question of the Four-Way Test and what it challenges us as Rotarians to do. As Sir Edmund himself said, "People do not decide to become extraordinary. They decide to accomplish extraordinary things."

SUMMARY

- This chapter took a deeper look into Question #3 — "Will it build GOODWILL and BETTER friendships?" This question involves a complex series of character traits, and those, like the Four-Way Test itself, need to work together to work properly. These character traits are Empathy, Caring/Compassion, Kindness and Respect.

- To develop and maintain positive relationships, you must have the ability to put yourself in the other person's shoes (Empathy) in order to properly evaluate whether something you say or do will have a positive (or negative) impact. "How would I like it if someone said/did that to me?" Also, you have to CARE about the effects of your actions on the other person, which means you have to CARE about the other person to begin with.

- Caring also involves Respect. Respect and Caring cause you to act with Kindness. That is why, in the example I shared in Chapter 2 on "Is it the TRUTH," you may believe, in truth, that the outfit does make your spouse look chunky. But Kindness, Respect and Caring are what keep you from being so tactless and hurtful to say it in just that way.

- Empathy — knowing how you'd feel in the other person's place — also keeps us from saying things that can have a negative effect on our relationships with others.

- We covered how respect for one another is the essential core of all of these related traits and that Rotarians have a unique opportunity in the world to reverse some of the incivility and rudeness in the world by continuing the visible application of Question #3.

• Finally, Compassion is that fundamental trait that takes what we feel—through Empathy and Kindness—and spurs us to respond. Again, it's because we CARE, that we want to help, particularly when someone is in need. We relate to the feeling of being in pain or distress and as kind, compassionate people, we reach out a hand to help.

YOUR TURN

The Third Question "Will it build GOODWILL and BETTER FRIENDSHIPS" is a great one to ponder and practice on a daily basis. Again, these are just a few ideas to get you started. It's great to get creative or to adapt them to your own experiences.

❑ What do you think your own personal "kindness level" is? Of course, everyone has better and worse days, but overall would others consider you to be a "kind person?" If so, how do you show that to the world? Are there areas you'd like to improve?

❑ The Random Acts of Kindness movement began as a book by Anne Herbert and grew as a grass-roots outreach. The Random Acts of Kindness Foundation (randomactsofkindness.org) is a non-profit organization that works to promote kindness in our communities, homes and schools. There is an "official" Random Acts of Kindness week on the calendar, but why should we limit this to just one week a year? Have fun—make it a regular practice to do something nice for someone who isn't expecting it. Buy a stranger a cup of coffee, help take packages out to a car, maybe take a few bunches of flowers or greeting cards to a nursing home for the residents...or the staff. It doesn't have to be a big or expensive gesture to make a difference.

❑ Because we are most comfortable with our family members, sometimes it's very easy to overlook kindness at home. When was the last time you told your spouse or significant other how much you really appreciate them?

Be specific — it's more meaningful that way. How about your children or parents? Have you done something notably kind for them lately? If you find you've been snappish or harsh in talking to them, maybe it's time to apologize for being abrasive? Let the people closest to you know how much they mean to you.

❑ Have you been putting off a phone call to someone you've been thinking of? Don't. Pick up the phone, take 15-20 minutes and catch up. Be sure to take time to *listen* to them. Being heard by another person is a huge kindness!

CHAPTER 5

QUESTION 4: WILL IT BE BENEFICIAL TO ALL CONCERNED?

"True greatness will be achieved through the abundant mind that works selflessly–with mutual respect, for mutual benefit."

— *Stephen Covey (Rotarian, Provo, UT)*

The fourth and final question in the Four-Way Test contains some elements we previously considered. It really expands the concepts of the previous three queries. It challenges us to consider how an interaction can lead to a positive outcome for all parties involved. The previously-discussed building block of Fairness is once again part of the equation, but so are new traits: Consideration and Cooperation.

Of all the questions, this one challenges us the most to consider the "whole picture" of the relationships we are dealing with. In this chapter, we'll take a look at how this final question serves to frame and complete the whole of the Four-Way Test. We will also explore how a tiny little word can have a major impact on our thoughts and actions.

FAIRNESS

fair (adj)
a: marked by impartiality and honesty: free from self-interest; b: conforming to established norms

If you recall in Chapter 3, we examined the notion of Fairness in light of Question #2. It's notable that two out of the four questions in the Four-Way Test are focused on Fairness. It once again points out how important it is to maintain a balance of needs when you are dealing with other people.

Chapter 3 does a more detailed breakdown of the singular trait of Fairness. In this section, however, I will discuss Fairness as it applies to *benefits*, which is really what Question 4 deals with.

Throughout history, we've been conditioned to believe that the normal outcome of any conflict is a "win-lose" scenario—one person wins, the other one loses. You can't have a winner without an at-least equal and opposite "loser." Too often, interactions or negotiations were a lot like "conflict resolution," in that you had to "win" in order to make a sale, form an alliance, or deliver a product.

But the implication that there always had to be some loser in the equation fell out of favor over time; it seemed too *predatory* somehow. So, in the 1980s a new style of negotiation became popular—that of the "win/win" scenario, one where both sides sought to benefit from a proposed transaction. "Win-win" was adopted by so many different sales and business philosophies that it practically became a religion, a much-chanted mantra for success.

But, that approach, too, was limited because it assumed you were only dealing with a two-sided transaction. This philosophy misses the point of true collaboration: creating something together that's bigger and better than what we can accomplish individually.

I'd like to suggest that we consider the mutual win, or what I'm calling the "win-win-win." What this means is, find that point where you can determine what the good is for you (increased sales, higher visibility, increased product/service awareness), what the good is for the other party (a new distribution channel, access to desired product/service) and then determine how both sides might benefit *jointly* from the offer. I think this is the true spirit of the "Fairness" proposed in Question 4 — it's about turning "What's in it for ME?" into "What's in it for US?" In order to do that, we have to turn to the next character trait: Consideration.

CONSIDERATION

consideration (n)
a: continuous and careful thought; b: thoughtful and sympathetic regard; c: an opinion obtained by reflection

Being considerate of others loops us right back to a fundamental root of pure kindness. It is basic civility that drives us to say something kind, or do something nice for others out of the sheer interest of another person's well-being. But, civility requires that we take an active interest in the needs, wants and desires of others. That *active* interest is where Consideration lives. It may seem like a circular argument but considerate people are more civil, they are intrinsically more compassionate, they are kinder, they tend to smile more often and lend a helping hand more often. As the Ragu tomato sauce commercial used to say, "It's all in there."

To dive more deeply into the meaning of Consideration, let's examine the dictionary definition more closely. Notice how definition (a) mentions "continuous and careful thought." There is conscious thought required. Yes, some people instinctively react with consideration, but frequently it requires thought, particularly if you are dealing in a situation where people are difficult or interactions are not in-balance. In definition (b) we recognize again the *thought* involved, but also point out that this is "sympathetic regard." We're back to that earlier building block of Empathy or "putting oneself in another's position." We are relating to what the other person wants, needs, or feels. Finally, (c) points out that the opinion—or conclusion or action—is obtained by reflection. It's *thinking* again, *considering*—in other words, being *thoughtful* in our *dealings with others*.

Infants and toddlers don't think. They need, want, demand. They are ego-driven, because it's how they survive. Over time, we are challenged to consider the needs of others, compromise, negotiate, and look for an agreeable solution. When we mature to the stage where we put the needs of others before our own—that's when we become considerate.

When I think about Consideration, I always recall the scene in the classic Star Trek movie, *The Wrath of Khan,* where First Officer Spock sacrifices his own life to save the rest of the crew of the Starship Enterprise. As he lays there dying, his explanation to his best friend Captain Kirk is simple: "The needs of the many outweigh the needs of the few... or the one."

COOPERATION

cooperation (n)
a: the actions of someone who is being helpful by doing what is wanted or asked for; common effort

Cooperation is the final building block in Question #4. It speaks to the idea of common effort toward a common good. When you examine the phrase "beneficial to all," we are talking precisely about common good, or at least "good in common," if the "good" isn't the same for each party. Cooperation does require a balance of feelings and treatment, however, particularly those involving Respect and Fairness. When people believe they are not being treated fairly, they may decide to "punish" the person they feel isn't treating them right by becoming uncooperative. So, you see once again that Fairness is forefront in having productive relationships.

The key to why Cooperation is so important to Question #4 is that it provides for efforts to be made on behalf of mutual benefit. As we saw in the previous section, the ideal scenario is a "win/win/win," where both sides benefit individually but then together create something bigger from the whole.

A New Dawn in Medicine through Cooperation

Dr. Charles H. Mayo (Rotary Club of Rochester, MN) was a firm believer in the power of Cooperation and demonstrated what can be accomplished when people work together for a common good. He, along with his brother Dr. William J. Mayo were formative in developing the Mayo Clinic, a world-renowned facility for medical care and research. Part of the success of the Mayo Clinic was the spirit of collaboration and cooperation Dr. Charles brought to it.

Charles was one of five children born into his family. His parents encouraged his education and provided him lessons in the arts, Latin and classic literature. Through his exposure to literature and stories his parents shared with him about their experiences in the Civil War and the Sioux Outbreak, he became sensitive to the plight of others. The Mayo's parents were instrumental in developing a sense of humanitarianism, pride in individual achievement and the power of cooperative effort. Both Charles and his brother William entered the medical profession with a goal of helping others.

Tragedy struck Rochester in 1883 in the form of a devastating tornado. Many buildings were damaged or destroyed and many residents were injured. Rochester had no hospital at that time, so the injured were treated at a temporary medical facility, led by Charles' brother William, assisted by the local nuns. This inspired the elder Mayo and his two sons to form the St. Mary's Hospital, which later grew into the Mayo Clinic, the first medical institution of its kind.

Originally the Clinic specialized in surgical procedures, which was the specialty of the two Mayo brothers. Over time, with collaboration by other physicians, and a strong belief in the value of sharing information with other medical facilities and physicians, the Clinic was able to expand its services, creating a unique integrated medical facility. This brought an increase in the number and types of patients supported. The Clinic developed a huge library of medical information and clinical records that were made available to any doctor that needed them, building a reputation of professional cooperation. In 1915, a joint venture with the University of Minnesota established the Mayo Foundation for Medical Education and Research, providing further educational facilities and programs for medical professionals around the world.

While the Mayo Clinic itself earned many accolades and awards, both Mayo brothers received individual recognition for their talents and accomplishments. Charles was made the head of the American Medical Association in 1906 and William was named to the Board of Regents of the University of Minnesota. They alternately also served as Chief Surgical Consultants to the U.S. Army during World War I. What started out as a 45-bed local hospital grew to a facility with over 1,000 employees today and over 4,500 physicians and scientists. The legacy left through the strong ethic of cooperation and compassion of the Mayo brothers not only helped their community, they left their stamp on the world for generations to come.

"ALL"—A LITTLE WORD THAT MEANS A LOT

While we are looking at the complete meaning and implications of Question #4, let's not overlook the smallest—but perhaps the most powerful—word in that statement. It's the word "all." It's the key to determining whether someone can honestly answer "yes" to Question #4: is each member in the equation benefiting in some way from the interaction?

We are not just discussing negotiations here. It can be something even simpler than that. Let's say there's something you are debating, telling someone you know. You've gone through the evaluation of whether it's the truth, etc. but at the end of the chain of questions you come up against the phrase "beneficial to all." Is there some positive result in telling the person what's on your mind? If the comment results in hurt feelings or a damaged relationship, then the point probably wasn't worth sharing or could have been delivered a different way. You may feel like you've benefited from getting something off your mind or "helped" someone by offering an objective critique, but if the other party isn't left with a positive "gain," then it wasn't "BENEFICIAL to all concerned."

If we stop to think about it, we are all essentially linked to varying degrees, for good or for ill. The British philosopher and Nobel Prize winner for Literature (1950), Bertrand Russell put it so well when he stated, "It's coexistence or no existence." If we don't have some level of compassion and concern for our fellow man, we don't have a "society" anymore...we have anarchy. Even the "least" of us deserves the same basic level of consideration, respect and care as the most wealthy and influential citizen on the planet.

There are many ways we can apply Question #4 to our lives — and most of those ways aren't that difficult. But, what about serving those who are literally outcasts in society? An all-women's Rotary Club in India, the Rotary Club of Jamshedpur Femina has adopted a nearby lepers' colony at Parvati Ghat as one of their community projects. Some of the services they provide the colony are mother and child health care, distribution of food and supplies, and artificial limbs to inmates who need them.

While we think of leprosy as an "ancient" and dwindling disease, the reality is that it's still rampant in several areas. Although the World Health Organization officially declared leprosy "eradicated" in 2005, nearly 130,000 people are diagnosed with leprosy in India every year, more than in any other country in the world. Although an effective cure for the disease has existed since the 1980s, the deep-rooted alienation and discrimination continues to impede the path from poverty to economic independence for individuals affected by the disease. Even once an individual is cured, they may still be banned from normal society because of the visible scars and deformities left behind by the disease. Rotarians who support and aid these leper colonies are providing vital services to those ostracized and shunned because of this horrible, disfiguring disease. They are doing this because it is truly "BENEFICIAL to all concerned."

Just three simple letters — "a-l-l" — can make the difference between being forgotten or being treated and respected as human. For those in need, they can be the difference between poverty and sustenance — even life and death. For us, they mean that Question #4 must be applied to everyone, at all times. Not just those people we think we can benefit from knowing or working with. Not just the people we like. Not just those who can offer us something. *EVERYONE — all the time.* Like the other three queries in the Four-Way Test, Question #4 does not judge, it does not discriminate. In the true spirit of Rotary, it is an essential part of our code of conduct, no matter what you are doing, with whom or where.

SUMMARY

- ◆ Question #4 of the Four-Way Test contains a number of character building blocks that challenge us to think broadly about our thoughts and conduct. Briefly, here's what we covered in this chapter.

- ◆ We took a second look at the virtue of Fairness. This trait first appeared in our examination of Question #2, and its reappearance here serves to highlight how important an equitable balance of interests is when developing and nurturing relationships.

- While the historical idea of a "win/lose" resolution in negotiations has certainly lost favor in light of the trendier "win/win" scenario, we looked at the idea of an even better way: that of "win/win/win" where both sides feel they have gained something individually, as well as jointly achieved something positive that they might not otherwise have been able to do.

- Overall, the traits in Question #4 challenge us to evaluation our interactions from the position of "What's in it for US?" instead of "What's in it for ME?" Consideration implies that we are giving careful thought to the needs and desires of others, not just what we want or expect.

- Cooperation is necessary when we are working toward a common benefit, as Question #4 directs us. Genuine cooperation can only exist when there is a real or perceived balance among participants. Studies have shown that people can become uncooperative as a way to hamper joint work when they feel they are not being treated fairly.

- Finally, when we look at the significance of Question #4 and what it is asking of us, it's important to notice that the smallest word in the phrase can actually be the most powerful. "ALL" means that we are expected to evaluate our thoughts and actions with everyone, at all times, regardless of what we are doing or with whom. Merriam-Webster defines "all" as "every member and individual component," so there is no distinction between who is deserving and who is not.

- Although it probably goes without saying, the word "all," also requires us to apply Question #4 with everyone we meet: Rotarians or not.

YOUR TURN

In this section, I offer a few ideas for putting Question #4—Will it be BENEFICIAL to all concerned?—to the test. Again, these are just a few things to think about—feel free to add your own twist or personalize them as you are inspired.

☐ The next time your children—or maybe nieces, nephews, grandchildren—raise the "It's not Fair!" cry, sit down with them to evaluate the situation before actually making a judgement on whether or not something is fair. What do they think isn't fair about the matter? What can or cannot be done about it? See if you can come up with an equitable "solution," even if it isn't one with a realistic or practical answer. For example, bad things do happen to good people and we can't really change that, but what would we want the "solution" to look like if we could?

☐ Challenge question: examine your attitude about the Four-Way Test and Question #4 when thinking about interactions with other Rotarians. Do you expect more from that interaction than you would, say, with a non-Rotarian? How do you treat a Rotarian differently from a non-Rotarian—or do you? Sometimes we hold more prejudice towards someone else who "should" be thinking/acting like us. Do you find yourself doing this?

☐ The next time you are working with or negotiating with someone, think about what a "win/win/win" scenario could look like. It doesn't have to be realistic or practical—sometimes the most impossible-looking solutions begin with a dream.

❑ In your Club or community, is there an area or group of people that may be underserved? Maybe it's not the most high-profile or glamorous cause, but is there someone you could be helping whose needs aren't being met? What can you do about it?

❑ It's never too soon to teach "service." Is there a project you or your Club might be able to take on in conjunction with a school, religious or social/sports club? Think about how you can share the idea of "BENEFICIAL to all" with the younger generation.

CHAPTER 6

MORE ABOUT INTEGRITY

"Have the courage to say no. Have the courage to face the truth. Do the right thing because it is right. These are the magic keys to living your life with integrity."
— W. Clement Stone (Rotarian, Chicago, IL)

Although we already examined the concept of Integrity in Chapter 2, that discussion treated the virtue as though it was only one singular thing. In this chapter, we will dissect this trait a bit further, showing that Integrity, in its completeness, really involves multiple character components, which all must work together to create the whole.

THE INTEGRITY TOOLBOX

In Chapter 2, we defined Integrity as "the adherence to a moral code or a code of values." That is certainly true and we used that definition to make the point in relation to Question #1—"Is it the TRUTH?" A second definition for Integrity is "the quality or state of being complete or undivided." It's this second meaning that we will look at more carefully in this section.

Integrity is a complex trait that, in reality, consists of four related concepts. These are

- ◆ Responsibility
- ◆ Reliability
- ◆ Courage
- ◆ Loyalty

We will be looking at each of these individually as this chapter progresses, but for now I want to focus on the idea of "completeness." The figure below is what I like to call the "Integrity Toolbox." It will be helpful for you to think of these individual character traits as the four tools in the Toolbox.

If we use the analogy of building a house, consider that each tool in the box is an important part of that construction. The hammer, saw, pencil and ruler all play necessary roles in making the house complete. Remove one tool, and you no longer have the capability of building that house. Without a saw, how can you cut lumber to length? Clearly, without a hammer, you have no way to secure boards and joists together. What about the pencil? Yes, you might be able to use a nail to score a length where you plan to make your cut, but you can't write down the measurements. Certainly, the ruler is a critical component to house-building success. In the same way, our *complete* house of Integrity requires that all four of our tools (Responsibility, Reliability, Courage and Loyalty) be used together, in sync and in line with their purpose, and with proper skill.

While actual tools need to be used in a particular order to ensure accuracy and success, the same is not true of the four components of Integrity. They do not need to be used in a specific order. So, with that, let's go on to discuss our first tool — the "ruler" — which we will call Responsibility.

RESPONSIBILTY

responsibility (n)

1: the quality or state of being responsible: such as

a : moral, legal, or mental accountability

b : reliability, trustworthiness

Responsibility is that trait that lets other people know we accept something or someone as ours. Generally, it refers to our ability to satisfactorily perform a task. But it can also refer to being answerable to a concept or philosophy. When we are responsible, we "own" a particular action, or are committed to a position or ideal. By fulfilling our obligations and commitments, people learn to trust that we are responsible and come to depend on that.

As humans, we learn responsibility largely based on a complex process of social expectation, experimentation and reinforcement. Not all cultures view responsibilities the same way. For example, in parts of the world, the women are solely responsible for making and maintaining the home and raising children. In other cultures, the responsibilities for these activities may be more evenly shared by both men and women. However, in most cultures, parents are primarily involved in teaching and enforcing responsibility appropriate to their cultural norms. The roles we fill as individuals, and as part of the larger culture, dictate the expectations for our behavior as productive, positive participants.

When we violate those expectations and act irresponsibly, by failing to keep a commitment or promise, for example, it damages our integrity. We are no longer keeping our part of the arrangement. If we go back to our definition of Integrity as "wholeness," by not being responsible, we find ourselves incomplete or divided. Part of our "toolbox" is out of alignment. And, if you recall from earlier chapters, we repeatedly discussed how relationships need to be "in balance," as part of the directives from the Four-Way Test.

Responsibility is a learned choice, a reflection of the social roles each of us assumes and values. Most people choose to practice and conform to the expectations of the roles they have accepted because they value the benefits and acknowledgements received. Responsibility is a vital part of Integrity because it keeps us in alignment with the expectations we have accepted and that other people have come to depend on.

RELIABILITY

reliability (n)
a: suitable or fit to be relied on; dependable

The characteristic of being depended on leads us directly to the virtue of Reliability. In looking at the root concept of this character trait, we find that to "rely" means to depend on for support, help or supply. A feature Reliability shares with Responsibility is that of *trust*. If you can be depended on, others know they can trust you to do what you said you would do, when you said you would do it.

As we discussed in Chapter 2, this notion of Trustworthiness is critical to developing long-term, productive and positive relationships because people want to know who they can count on. Unpredictable behavior ruins the possibility of developing a steady relationship—most of us want to connect with and trust dependable people.

Put that to the test: if you needed someone's assistance or support, would you choose someone you knew to be reliable and trustworthy, or would you go to the person who regularly "flakes out" on you? If it was for something that mattered, you certainly would choose the steadier of the two options, right?

How do Integrity and Reliability relate? Think of it this way: Reliability means being able to depend that a person or system will perform and maintain its functions in routine circumstances, as well as in unexpected conditions. Integrity, then, is consistency between one's actions, values, methods, measures and principles. If we go back to the toolbox illustration we were using earlier, think of Reliability as the mark you leave with your pencil—can it be trusted to be accurate and true?

COURAGE

courage (n)
mental or moral strength to venture, persevere, and withstand danger, fear, or difficulty

To continue with our toolbox metaphor, Courage is the saw. When you are about to make a cut, you must be committed. You have to trust in the rightness of the mark. Putting the saw to the work is no time for doubt. It's about being firm in your convictions.

Likewise, it's not always easy to demonstrate courage. Fortunately, many of us do not face truly difficult decisions—those involving life or death—which call upon us to make judgements involving integrity. But, there are circumstances that require us to take a deep breath and hold true to what's right, even when it might be tempting just to give in and take the easier path.

That's where Courage comes in. As the definition explains, Courage involves "mental or moral strength" to overcome danger, fear or difficulty. It's not, as we often think, the *lack of fear*. We all have things we are afraid of. That's normal, and healthy in many cases. Courage involves working through that fear, to stick with what we know is right, for our good—and often the good of others.

The Courage part of Integrity comes when we must stand up for what is right, when we are afraid of the possible outcome.

Sometimes that fear is virtual—we don't have to actually have fear of physical repercussions. Instead, we are worried about what someone else will think about us or maybe that we'll lose popularity, friendship or business standing. But, recall our discussions in the previous chapter about being "beneficial to all concerned." Sacrificing your integrity can never pass Question #4 in the Four-Way Test. If we are looking for a "win/win" by making a bad choice, it'll never happen. At a minimum, you are the loser by violating your integrity. It may not be easy to stand true to your convictions—assuming you are in the right—but it's better than letting yourself down.

Sometimes living true to your integrity *does* involve risk to yourself in a potentially more dangerous way. In the next section, we'll meet a young woman who takes great risks to assist others who have no other champion, and her courageous commitment to do what's right is an amazing story.

Courage of Convictions
Heroines are born from necessity and this is how a Rotarian—who will be known as Evin to protect her identity—became the champion for the rights of the Yizidi and Syrian refugees in Kurdistan. Evin is a woman of courage who became the mouthpiece of nameless women suffering under the brutal rule of the Islamic State. As she says, very few people in the world know the different wars people in Kurdistan (which includes groups in parts of Turkey, Iraq, Syria and Iran) are involved in. Amidst these raging conflicts, human rights abuses abound with minorities like the Yizidis—and by extension the Kurds. They suffer from acts of genocide at the hands of the Islam State because they, the Yizidis, are considered "devil worshippers."

Evin is a human rights activist. She got involved because she wanted to tell the stories of women suffering from the atrocities of a war waged by a sadistic group determined to eradicate minorities like the Yizidis. Their activities in Sinjar Province in Northern Iraq, where men and older women were murdered and buried in mass graves, while younger women were auctioned as sex slaves when ISIS captured the town, are evidence of their hatred.

Evin fought and got into the Rotary Fellowship because she knew it would give her tools to positively impact the lives of the refugees. Although Iraq had no Rotary Club, she used her resourcefulness to get the Rotary Club in Asuncion, Paraguay to sponsor her. At the Rotary Peace Center in Bangkok, she stood out among other talented individuals because of her quiet, frank and eager-to-learn manner. This fellowship was very important because Evin could share experiences with people from all over the world, some of whom had seen some form of brutal conflict like she had.

The suffering that the Islamic State has visited on people in Northern Iraq and Syria cannot be imagined. Chilling narratives of rape, torture and trauma characterize these stories. Yet women and girls who have lived these realities and come out alive still wish to share their experiences. Unfortunately, most foreign journalists do not fully grasp the extent of the danger. Sometimes they accidentally reveal images of these women that result in their families, still under ISIS rule, to be tortured and killed. Working as a translator, Evin endeavors to ensure that the identities of these women are protected while their stories are heard.

Evin herself has lost relatives in the conflict; she recounts that "murder and killing are a normal part of life here." Her little cousin and her young nephew, with whom she shared a special relationship, were killed in Syria. He was killed while helping the Kurds to fight ISIS in Syria. To her, his sacrifice was not in vain; even though she is saddened by his death, she understands that ISIS must be contained.

Being courageous is a responsibility that Evin did not ask for but she undertakes because of her desire to protect an already battered people. She lives in a world in which murder and killings are normalized. A world in which women are sold as property and spoils of war. A world in which women are objectified and their bodies violated by an evil fanatical group that seeks to eradicate minorities.

Evin's job is a dangerous and precarious one. She is not safe from the repercussions of ISIS, so attempts to communicate with the outside world must be done through an alias. She is a heroine who does not want to be named, but stands out through her valiant acts of selflessness and courage. She has taken upon herself a specific mission: to tell the stories of courageous, nameless women so that the world can intervene and end these atrocities.

LOYALTY

loyalty (n)
the quality or state or an instance of being loyal (which we can define as a feeling of strong support for someone or something)

The final tool in our Toolbox is our hammer, representing Loyalty. When you are working with wood, nothing is as comforting as your trusty hammer. You can count on your hammer to perform predictably when used properly and there's nothing really complicated about its actions.

Similarly, Loyalty itself is a relatively "black or white" condition: either you have loyalty, or you do not. You can't be "somewhat loyal" because, by definition, if you are not consistent in your allegiance to a person or a situation, you cannot be considered loyal.

Loyalty is another one of those character traits crucial to building and maintaining relationships. Like several of the other traits we have looked at already, Loyalty expects Dependability. But, we have to be smart in giving and receiving loyalty: loyalty should not be blind.

Consider the argument of which is more important, loyalty or integrity? There are times where people would argue that loyalty is the most important trait, that you need to stick with your family, business, or community, no matter what.

But what if the group you are being loyal to isn't behaving ethically? For example, you could certainly make the point that violent street gangs show an immense loyalty to one another, and to the gang as a whole. But is that a good place in which to place your loyalty? It can certainly be very difficult to turn away from such a "community" and take a position of integrity. But loyalty to any person or group that behaves immorally or illegally puts your own integrity at risk.

Because our culture leans much more strongly towards moral relativism, it seems easier to defend positions of questionable loyalty. But, there are basic "truths" that exist regardless of how we might want to justify differently. Recall from the discussion in Chapter 2, a "truth" exists because it means something that's true. And, "truth" is universal. For example, it's wrong to hurt people and it's right to take care of them. It's wrong to steal and right to allow others to have their own possessions. Cheating is wrong, but being fair is right. This is "true" no matter what.

One may not always correctly decide who to be loyal to, and some people may even disappoint us or deceive us when we are loyal to them. Despite all this, Loyalty always allows us to be true to ourselves and to our values. And true loyalty must also include the quality of Integrity, because without being true to ourselves, our beliefs and principles, we cannot be true to someone else.

INTEGRITY AND ETHICS

So far in this book, we have looked at words that seem to be interchangeable. But we have come to see that, while they may be similar, and used as though they were the same, in breaking down their actual meaning we have found subtle, but important, differences. Integrity and Ethics are another pair of words that are frequently substituted for one another, but they do have slightly different meanings, as we will see in this section.

As we begin with the discussion of the differences between the two, let's look at the definitions of the words. According to Merriam-Webster, ethics (the plural noun) is "a set of moral issues or aspects (as rightness)." In other words, it's about following rules. Note the definition does specify "moral issues," but basically, it's still about keeping to a set of requirements. Integrity, as we saw earlier, is about doing the right thing, regardless of what the rules say. Ethics is more externally focused, then, where integrity refers more to an internal condition.

So, the question arises: can you be ethical but still not have integrity? Of course! Let's say someone in business is conforming to a set of company rules because they don't want to get in trouble—not fraternizing romantically with co-workers or perhaps outside vendors, for example,—because such behavior could lead to favoritism or "kick-backs." But, if those rules weren't in place, someone with lesser integrity might go ahead and act on those tendencies, because there's nothing "ethically" stopping them.

Another way to look at it is this: if we say that "ethics" is like our tax code, while some are strictly keeping to the rules of the code, others are looking to get around it as much as they can, using loopholes and shelters to avoid paying their fair share. A simpler analogy is that Ethics is like staying within the lines when you're coloring; Integrity is still being able to create a positive work of art when there aren't any lines to constrain you.

In closing, Integrity is all about doing the right thing when no one else is looking. It's your CHARACTER that keeps you obeying life's moral rules. As Rotarian Harold S. Kushner (Natick, MA) is quoted to say, "There is no right way to do a wrong thing."

SUMMARY

- In this section, we took a deeper look at those "tools" in the Integrity Toolbox: Responsibility, Reliability, Courage and Loyalty. We assigned tools as individual metaphors for the essential tools in the box, all of which need to work together to build our "house of Integrity."

- Responsibility is all about being accountable for an action or task, while we defined Reliability as being dependable. What this means is, when we accept Responsibility for something, Reliability means we can be counted on to do it. Responsibility and Reliability work together as the "ruler" or the measuring stick along with the pencil that is there to leave evidence of the "mark" or commitment.

- Courage, then, is the saw in the toolbox. Courage is not the absence of fear, rather, it is the ability to overcome fear and move through it. It is the "cut" in the process of building the house. We commit to what we know is good and right and persevere in spite of doubt and obstacles.

- As we saw in the story of "Evin," it takes Courage sometimes to take a stand for what's right. While Evin certainly has much to fear from the danger she puts herself in by supporting women and families in the face of the ISIS conflict, she perseveres in spite of the risk to herself personally because she is standing up for those who cannot stand for themselves.

- When we explored the idea of Loyalty, we used the fourth tool in the box—the hammer—as the metaphor. Loyalty is a condition that must be used with thought and consideration; blind loyalty can lead you to be "true" to someone or something lacking in integrity. Loyalty can't be *true* loyalty without Integrity.

- Finally, we explored the idea of Integrity vs. Ethics. We saw that Ethics pertains to adhering to rules and generally expected behaviors, but that Integrity really means sticking to what's right even when the "rules" might say otherwise. Ethics may provide an external mechanism meant to enforce doing the right thing. Integrity is doing the right thing even when those restraints aren't present.

YOUR TURN

This chapter covered four very important character traits: Responsibilty, Reliability, Courage and Loyalty. In this section, I offer a few points to ponder as we think about how to incorporate Integrity into our lives.

- ❑ Ask yourself how likely you are, in varying situations, to push the boundaries of rules or ethics? Is it a big deal to take a few pencils or pens from work? How about borrowing the company car to run a few personal errands? This is not meant to be judgmental, rather directed to raising awareness to everyday ethical "oopses."

- ❑ Courage does not mean "lack of fear." Everyone is afraid of *something*. Maybe it's heights. Perhaps you are afraid of spiders, loud noises, or walking alone in the dark. It could also be more serious — fear of financial distress, fear of losing a loved one. Make a list of your fears and assess how likely they are to happen, and what the possible outcome is. Consider if there's something you can do to lessen the fear or the likelihood your fear will be realized. Power is in working through and overcoming fears. (This is a *great* exercise to share with children or young people.)

- ❑ Where does your loyalty lie? Think about who or what you are loyal to: a family member, a boss, a political party, a religion. Is that loyalty deserved or do you question it sometimes? Maybe share the question "Is loyalty or integrity more important" with a group of friends, your Rotary Club, or a group of young people, and see what answers you get.

❏ How does it feel when loyalty is either not returned, or someone you felt loyalty to disappoints you? What lesson do you learn from that?

❏ What do you think about the quote "There's no right way to do a wrong thing?" Agree/disagree? Why or why not? (Again, this is a great question to share with youth and kids.)

CHAPTER 7

TOLERANCE VS. ACCEPTANCE

"If we cannot end now our differences, at least we can help make the world safe for diversity."

— *John F. Kennedy (Rotary Club of Hyannis, MA)*

This chapter is unique in that the ideals of Tolerance and Acceptance are not strictly called out by the Four-Way Test, but to truly stick to the spirit of the Test, they are building blocks that must be present. While "tolerance" is in vogue these days, I'd like to present the idea that it isn't entirely the shining concept it's made out to be. Further, how does Acceptance figure into our Clubs and our communities, particularly at a time where so much of humanity seems to be at odds? This is what this chapter is all about.

TOLERANCE

tolerance (n)
a : sympathy or indulgence for beliefs
or practices differing from or conflicting
with one's own
b : the act of allowing something

Over the past several years, one of the big buzzwords has been "Tolerance." We are advised to be "tolerant," to "teach tolerance,"—there's even a Museum of Tolerance! Religious tolerance, gender tolerance, cultural tolerance...you name it, we are expected to "tolerate." But what is this "tolerance" we are preaching anyway? Because this is such a big topic in our schools these days, I'd like to turn again to concepts we offer our schools and students as part of the SocialSmarts' "Exploring the Virtues" curriculum. In the "Tolerance vs. Acceptance" lesson in Virtues I, we drill down into these two concepts and really get to what they mean, and how they affect us.

Of course, in order to understand it, we have to define it first. In the "lower grades" version of the lesson, we use the following:

Tolerance: Putting up with something or someone different from what we are used to.

This is an interesting point: when you stop to think about it, each and every one of us is "different" in some way. Maybe it's our background, where we came from, how we grew up. Maybe I have a college education but some of the people I hang out with don't. I like gardening, others are into remote-control planes. I have blue eyes and brown hair; my best friend is blonde. I mean, we are ALL different. To make this point to our young students, we suggest the class create a "differences chart" that illustrates, by varying characteristics how no two students (or include the teacher if you like) have exactly the same set of characteristics.

This is all good, but it's only the FIRST step in the lesson. Notice that Tolerance, by definition, means we are "putting up with" others in spite of their differences. "You're different, but I'll deal with it, in spite of your differences." It's like saying that we, ourselves, are the yardstick for "normal." *You* are different; *I* am the norm. And, because I'm a great person who is politically correct by being TOLERANT, I'll put up with those differences.

While we are on the subject of "political correctness," there's a real problem with that concept as well. While it seems to mean that it's important for us to be sensitive to the viewpoints, perspectives and opinions of others, it actually has come to be a not-so-subtle form of bullying. Being "politically correct" has been taken to the point of ridiculousness. It frequently means that I expect YOU to be sensitive to my needs and position, to communicate and behave in such a fashion that you don't offend *me*. If you lack this sensitivity, then you are being intolerant and are clearly a less-evolved individual.

This puts the burden on the other person, to be careful and cautious with their own viewpoints and communications, regardless of their opinions. Expressing themselves within their own frame of reference may be considered unsympathetic, inconsiderate, racist or worse. It's a completely one-sided approach. It assumes only one side has the right perspective, not that both sides need to be tolerant of each other.

I also personally struggle with the phrase "indulgence" in the Merriam-Webster definition of Tolerance. To drill down to what "indulge" means, we see the definition is "to treat with excessive leniency, generosity, or consideration." So, if we use that explanation, being "tolerant" means we are being "excessively considerate?" That smacks of condescension to me, which is *exactly* what much of today's tolerance is all about. "I may not like you, but I'll put up with you because I am expected to."

So, tolerance may be the state of where we recognize and consider others' differences, which is an important first step. But I would like to suggest that it's not enough.

ACCEPTANCE

acceptance (n)
1: the quality or state of being accepted or acceptable
2: the act of accepting something or someone: the fact of being accepted

But, if Tolerance isn't enough, where do we go from here? Let's take the concept a step further and move to "Acceptance." Using the same SocialSmarts lesson, we explain that Acceptance is...

Approving of something (or someone) and treating it as normal, right, or included.

By this definition, Acceptance means that I consider you to be just as normal and "right" as I am. Differences aside, when I am accepting, I include you and welcome you. It comes, partially, from the understanding that we have more in common that we have differences. I may have a particular gender orientation and you have a different one, but, ultimately, we are both wanting the same thing: love, understanding, and to be caring and cared by someone who matters to us. I may believe in one form of religion or spirituality and you may believe something very different. But as a rule, we are trying to live a decent, positive life where we don't intentionally hurt others. And, who am I to say whether your way or mine is "more right?" Just because I don't agree or don't practice what you do, it doesn't make you "inferior" or "wrong."

If you examine what "accepted" means, you'll find this as a definition: "regarded favorably: given approval." This is quite different from just "putting up with." I am seeing you and reacting to you in a positive light. I recognize and accept you for who you are, not just catalog your sets of real or perceived differences.

There's another issue when it comes to the difference between Tolerance and Acceptance. And, it's a VERY important distinction. You see, no matter who we are or how hard we try, at some point in our lives we are going to meet someone whom we don't like, or with whom we don't agree. We may have to work with them and get along with them. If we don't learn to be patient with other people's differences, we just won't be able to co-exist.

The Power of the Pen Against Intolerance

In the North Carolina countryside of the 1950s, two brave newspapermen took a stand against bigotry. Columbus Country, NC was plagued by the terrorism of the Ku Klux Klan. Rotarians Willard G. Cole (Whilteville, NC) and W. Horace Carter (Tabor City, NC) were determined to stop them. In opposing the Klan, both journalists put themselves in positions of real danger. The Klan's acts of intolerance against those who stood up against them included cross burning, floggings, even murder. Carter represented the weekly *Tabor City Tribune,* with a 1,700 copy audience, while Cole published the *Whiteville News Reporter,* a semi-weekly paper whose circulation numbered around 5,000.

For over three years, the two used their journalistic skills and editorial position to write about the Klan's events, exposing their hateful acts, even going so far as to attend actual Klan meetings and reporting on them. As you can imagine, this did not go over well with the Klan, who threatened the newspapermen, their sources and the papers' advertisers regularly.

Cole and Carter were after information that could be used in court against the Klan, and they were finally able to gain the evidence that was needed. As an interesting note, the position the journalists were taking against the Klan was not met with broad community support, likely due to fear of Klan reprisal. Undeterred, the men persisted in their crusade and continued to publish editorials.

Because of the reporting efforts of the two Rotarians, the FBI got involved in the investigation. Eventually the leader of the local Klan, "Grand Dragon" Thomas Hamilton, and several Klan members were convicted on both state and Federal charges. The terrorism ceased. TV legend Edward R. Murrow actually brought cameras to Columbus Country to film his famous show, "See it Now," which also included footage from a special Rotary meeting that was held to honor the two men.

Filmmaker Walt Campbell later made a documentary *The Editor and the Dragon: Horace Carter Fights the Clan* sharing Carter's account of his newspaper's efforts and his personal conflict with the Carolina Klansmen. In 1953, both the *Tribune* and the *Whiteville News Reporter* were awarded the Pulitzer Prize for Public service, citing "their successful campaign against the Ku Klux Klan, waged on their own doorstep at the risk of economic loss and personal danger, culminating in the conviction of over one hundred Klansmen and an end to terrorism in their communities."

These two Rotarians used the tools they had at hand to wage a campaign to stop intolerance and hatred in their community. In spite of the personal threats they faced, both men courageously stood up for what was right, raised awareness of the evil in their midst, and persisted until the Klan had been stopped.

TOLERANCE IS PASSIVE, ACCEPTANCE IS NOT

But, merely "co-existing" in the same space really isn't enough. As we saw, Tolerance really refers to just "putting up" with something or someone, even if we don't like it/them. It's a passive state—one that keeps us stuck in the same spot. We explain to students that it's the same thing as when we say, "Ok, I will if I have to." But it's clear we really don't like it. Tolerance is a state that focuses on our *differences*. It's about allowing something, but it not necessarily something we're happy with.

Being accepting, on the other hand, is an active state, where we not only understand and tolerate someone's differences, but we appreciate them and value them. Acceptance recognizes that while we are different, we probably have more things in common than we have differences. Often those differences complement each other. Acceptance gives us forward movement; it brings people closer together by making room for different experiences, perspectives, abilities and opinions.

As we have done throughout this book, we look at the character traits we are discussing in light of others we have previously covered. In this case, Tolerance is, in a way, another form of patience. But Acceptance requires not only patience, but empathy, which, in turn, requires understanding that as different as we may be, we're basically the same in what we want, what we need, and in our inalienable rights to want those things. It's where we get back to Fairness and Equality, which we covered in Question #2. It's about the Respect, Empathy and Compassion that Question #3 brought up. It really is about "all," whenever we deal with people.

So, while "Tolerance" seems to be what everyone is aiming for, I would like to put forth that this isn't enough. While we probably won't always get along at all times, we can certainly strive to be more accepting and understanding of others, regardless of where they come from and who they are. Often, we'll find that we are more and better together, because of the different perspectives, life experiences and personalities we bring to the table. By accepting, we can work to find the "win/win/win," because it really is all about "us."

Olympic Gold While Bridging Two Cultures

An example of how powerful the idea of Acceptance is, we have only to look at one man who successfully and seamlessly represented two cultures. Duke Kahanamoko, the "Father of Modern Surfing" (Rotary Club of Honolulu, HI) is notable not just for his accomplishments, but also for how he came to be the legendary swimmer and surfer we applaud him for.

Duke Paoa Kahinu Mokoe Hulikohola Kahanamoko was born in 1890, to a family that, while not officially part of the ruling family, was once deeply rooted in the traditional Hawaiian monarchy. He was named "Duke" after his father, who was first given the name because he was born during an 1869 visit by the Duke of Edinburgh. When young Duke was just a child, the reigning Queen was overthrown, ushering a new era of American occupation and rule. Although his entire culture was being subjugated, Duke bore no outward ill-will toward the new government. Rather, he worked diligently to win himself a spot on the US Olympic team preparing for the 1912 games. As it turned out, this young man was the only Hawaiian on the team. He persevered despite being referred to as one of the poor "brown naked kids" who would swim through tropical waters to harvest a few meager coins thrown to them by wealthier travelers. Duke's success at the Olympics earned him fame as "the greatest swimmer the world of sport has ever seen."

Well, after winning five Olympic medals in swimming, Duke moved to Southern California, where he began a career as an actor. At the same time, he worked to promote the sport of surfing. In 1925, while he was in California, he participated in rescuing eight men who were floundering after a 40-foot vessel capsized, putting all 29 passengers in the water. Duke made three trips out on his surfboard to complete the rescue.

But, in spite of his fame, Duke was not immune from prejudice by the white majority. Because of his dark Hawaiian skin, he was once turned away from a restaurant in a small town in the Southern California mountains, as he arrived with a group of swimmers. The restaurant told him, "We don't serve Negroes here."

At the same time he became more entrenched in celebrity through films, surfing expeditions and evangelizing the sport of surfing over all, Duke continued to embrace his heritage. Once, when President Franklin Roosevelt paid the islands an official visit, Duke, dressed up as King Kamehameha the Great, paddled out in an outrigger canoe to meet him. Later in life, Duke became a military police officer, civil law enforcement officer, and later, served as Sherriff of Honolulu.

As his legacy, Duke became the first person to be inducted in the Swimming Hall of Fame and the Surfing Hall of Fame. He was made Hawaii's Official Greeter in acknowledgment of all he did to promote the state's culture and traditions. There are still any number of events and establishments bearing his name, in recognition of the impact he has had on the world through his abilities. The Duke Kahanamoku Surfing Championships are named in his honor. The famous Hawaiian crooner Do Ho used to perform in a hall bearing Duke's name. Legendary beachfront and waterfront bars and restaurants such as "Duke's Waikiki" and an entire chain of restaurants in Washington, California, Hawaii and Florida all carry the "Duke's" name. In 2002, the US Postal Service honored Duke on what would have been his 112th birthday by issuing a commemorative stamp.

Rather than allow the changes in his native state to demoralize him and hold him back, Duke accepted the dawn of a new government and a new way of doing things. In so doing, he gained acceptance and appreciation the world over. In working to promote surfing and the Hawaiian cultural traditions, he stood as a human bridge and ambassador between two cultures, preserving what might otherwise have been lost.

As Rotarians, we already belong to an immense family that always has our core beliefs and practices in common. No matter where you are, when you step into a Rotary meeting, you are accepted as a brother or sister. As best-selling author, J.K. Rowling has said, "Differences of habit and language are nothing at all if our aims are identical and our hearts are open."

SUMMARY

♦ This Chapter focused on the ideas of Tolerance and Acceptance. While these words are often interpreted to mean the same thing, in reality they have significant differences.

♦ Tolerance is the idea of "putting up with" people or things that are different than we expect or have come to find as "normal." While it seems to imply that there is an understanding, in fact tolerance draws attention to *differences* between people but doesn't do much to build common ground.

♦ Acceptance, on the other hand, is the idea that something different can contribute to a greater understanding to the world as we see it or some other benefit. Acceptance is about recognizing that, while we may have differences, our varying experiences, perspectives, cultures and more may actually complement each other and, together, create something greater than just its individual parts.

♦ Tolerance is a passive state where we are *allowing* something in spite of differences. Acceptance, in contrast, is an active condition where we appreciate and value both the differences that may exist as well as the commonality we share.

♦ Tolerance can also give way to concepts such as "political correctness," which, can actually become a form of bullying meant to suppress opinions and viewpoints of others under the mantle of being "intolerant."

♦ As we saw in the story of Duke Kahanamoku, Acceptance can be an effective tool to promote and develop greater understanding between cultures. The Duke used his native abilities as a swimmer and a surfer to adapt himself to a changing world. He also used his personal success as a platform to bring awareness and appreciation for ancient, traditional cultures.

• As Rotarians, we have a unique position in that we are already, by virtue of belief and practice, part of a large, global family. Differences in culture, language, custom don't matter because our commonalities are greater—and stronger—than our differences.

YOUR TURN

This chapter provided a detailed examination of the concepts of Tolerance and Acceptance. To develop a deeper understanding of their differences, these points may serve as an interesting starting point for dialog and perhaps, even, changes in practice.

- ❏ Our current culture seems to one of increasing divisiveness. In your community, how committed do you think people are to Tolerance? How about Acceptance? What are some of the challenges you see in your neighborhoods and what could you do to change that?

- ❏ In the interest of Tolerance, what are some topics you might be cautious about—or even completely avoid—discussing in settings such as the workplace, a dinner party or evening out with a group, even perhaps your own Rotary Club?

- ❏ Do you personally see incidents of discrimination or intolerance where you live, work, or play? Have you taken steps to address it or call attention to it? Why or why not?

- ❏ What can you do to open the topic of Tolerance and Acceptance to our children and youth? This is a great time to get into a discussion about bullying because this type of treatment is often the end-result of intolerance. What do you think our children learn from the intolerance, hate-speak, and flat-out bullying seen today, even from our country's leaders, on TV, in newspapers, in social media and more? How do we expect our young people to avoid bullying when they see it modeled daily in the adults in their lives?

❑ If the concept of Tolerance is inadequate, what can you do to move it to the next level of Acceptance? Can you propose a local or civic day of "Acceptance" to promote awareness?

CHAPTER 8

APPLICATION OF THE FOUR-WAY TEST

"When you see a want, supply it. When you see a defect, correct it. When you hear a call for help, answer it."

— *James F. Conway, Rotary International President (1969-1970), Sun City, AZ*

In the preceding chapters, we have looked at each of the Questions in the Four-Way Test individually. The goal of examining them independently was to gain a better understanding of the meaning and intent behind each one. The purpose of this chapter is to combine them into their one, unifying whole. How can we apply the Four-Way Test — and other complementary beliefs of Rotary — to make the changes, both small and large, that we have come to expect from its members?

THE MOST IMPORTANT QUESTION IS...?

As I was working on the separate chapters dedicated to each one of the Questions in the Four-Way Test, I decided to ask a question of my Rotarian network: "Of the four questions in the Four-Way

Test, which one do you think is most important, and why?" I was very surprised and pleased by the number of responses I received. I was particularly impressed by the caliber of responses.

The first wave of responses from my own personal network was interesting. Everyone had a very distinct view on which question was the most important. Here are a few of the responses I received:

"For me it's truth. Not to tell the truth is unfair, it's a lie."

"The most important one to me is 'is it fair to all concerned.' I believe if everyone on this planet followed this basic rule 'is it fair to all concerned' there wouldn't be any wars, racism or discrimination based on religion or sexuality, people wouldn't abuse other people and children would be safe at school or the park. 'Is it fair to all concerned' seems so simple to me."

"I will go with 'Will it Build Goodwill and Better Friendships?' The number one reason people stay in Rotary is friendship/ fellowship. If we are going to do more good work and continue building a strong organization for another 100 years, it will clearly be because we allowed friendship to transcend our differences."

I thought I'd tally the responses and see what the numbers showed. Here are the results of my first poll:

Q1: Is it the TRUTH   57%

Q2: Is it FAIR   29%

Q3: Will it build GOODWILL   14%

Q4: Will it be BENEFICIAL   0%

One club member wrote me and said he thought my question was a very intriguing one, and he thought he'd bring it to HIS club and see what his membership thought. Their results were a little different.

Q1: Is it the TRUTH   51%

Q2: Is it FAIR   18%

Q3: Will it build GOODWILL   3%

Q4: Will it be BENEFICIAL   28%

Some of the comments I got back were:

"Is it the TRUTH: If your actions are based on truth, and your actions become your integrity and your character in all things—when you look at things honestly you can see your true self & be open to see other people's honesty and open to their point of view—not just your own."

"Will it be beneficial to all concerned: Because it is of the upmost importance that consideration be made that all concerned are to benefit rather than only certain individuals with certain interests."

"Is it fair: The truth is sometimes unfair and sharing the truth is not always fair."

I was so excited that another Rotarian had taken this question to their club! But that was only the beginning. Then, out of the blue, I receive an email from the e-Club of South Africa One which has members from the USA, Tanzania, Qatar, the UK, and South Africa.

Here are the results they came up with over a multi-week period (they asked members on two different occasions. The columns below represent first week's results, then the second, and finally the average.

Q1: Is it the TRUTH	30%	40%	35%
Q2: Is it FAIR	30%	10%	20%
Q3: Will it build GOODWILL	10%	20%	15%
Q4: Will it be BENEFICIAL	30%	30%	30%

The comments that accompanied the poll included:

"'Is it the Truth' is the most important. Because if you can't be truthful then it is almost impossible to truly follow the other 3."

"I believe No 2 is the most important. It is very difficult for everything that one does to be BENEFICIAL to all concerned and what one thinks, says and does although FAIR, may not lead to BETTER FRIENDSHIPS. At times things one says may not be the TRUTH for very good ethical reasons. So as long as it is FAIR it is OK by me."

"Will it build GOODWILL and BETTER FRIENDSHIPS. This is one of the most important to me when applied to my personal relationships—Will it build goodwill? i.e. long term—will it be worth winning the "argument" as it may change the course of your future relationships e.g. my very difficult daughter-in-law."

To date I've had several contacts from clubs across the world asking if they can use my newsletter in their clubs for meetings. These clubs inspired me to turn this into a challenge: "The Most Important Question Challenge." I'd love to spur more reflection on the individual questions in the Four-Way Test and see what members come up with. I have committed to creating a page on the book's website to record and share Rotarians' responses, both on an individual level and more broadly. It'll be interesting to see how the results develop over time. If you decide to use this Challenge with your Club or maybe even a Rotaract or Interact group, please drop me an email with the results. You can find my contact info in the back of the book, but for convenience, I'm at corinne@corinnegregory.com.

ALL OR NONE

But, of course, this test is known as the Four-Way Test, and the reality is, while we can consider each test singly, in order to pass the Test we need to apply all four.

By starting at Question #1, "Is it the TRUTH?" we may find ourselves in a challenging spot. As we explored in Chapter 2, the Truth can be very subjective. Increasingly, the "truth" is whatever a person chooses to believe or feels is relevant. But, as we saw, there are certain sets of "big truths"—what Stephen Covey calls the "true north truth"—that are more universally true than related to one's own perception of truth.

The slippery slope of relative truth is becoming even more slippery with younger generations. As Marty Lindeman, with the Rotary Club of Needham, MA shared in his email response to "The Most Important Question...,"

> *"The two youngest generations in our midst usually describe truth as 'What I feel and say it is.' Tomi Lahren, a teenage internet blogger who this week is in her 15 minutes of fame on liberal talk shows says 'I speak my truth. If you don't like it, tough. I will always be honest and stand in my truth.' That's ethical quicksand, or good old fashioned situational ethics.*

If Rotarians follow that path, the Four-Way Test is worthless right from the first paragraph. Admittedly, the discussion of truth in Rotary clubs is usually pretty spotty in my experience. The value of the Four-Way Test is using it to stimulate awareness and further thinking and discussion. It is part of the "pattern" or rubric of ethical thinking of Rotarians if it is used within the thousands of Rotary clubs around the world. While the four parts are somewhat redundant, it does function best when applied as a whole."

That is exactly the point. The Four-Way Test needs to be applied as a whole. As comments above showed, while some Rotarians may believe that one of the questions is more foundational than others, they agree that they all need to work. Similar to an old-fashioned "Truth Table" if you can't check all the boxes as a "yes," then, by definition, the whole test fails.

Let me give you a simple but classic example. Your spouse/partner/significant other asks you the immortal question "Does this outfit make me look fat?" You mentally go racing through your Four-Way Test Checklist. Depending on how you answer, you may be telling the TRUTH, and it may be FAIR, but you can bet your last dollar that your answer won't be building any GOODWILL, right? And, I'm not sure where anyone benefits. Not only does your answer fail the Four-Way Test, but it could be a failure you won't live down for YEARS!

SERVICE ABOVE SELF

Along with the Four-Way Test, there is another motto that is a hallmark of Rotary, that of "Service Above Self." Just like the

Four-Way Test, this fundamental statement has evolved over the course of many years to be what it is today.

As early as 1911, Rotary approved the phrase "He Profits Most Who Serves Best" during the second National Convention of Rotary held in Portland, OR. Rotarian Arthur Sheldon had coined a version of that saying at the first National Convention, the previous year. At the Portland convention, while on a convention-based boating event, Ben Collins, at the time was President of the Minneapolls, MN club, shared with another Seattle based Rotarian, J.E Pinkham, a standard that his club was using, the idea of "Service, Not Self." Pinkham, impressed by Collins' saying, invited Paul Harris who was also on the trip to join the conversation. Harris subsequently asked Collins to share the motto in an address to the convention where it was enthusiastically welcomed.

Despite the popularity of both phrases, it took nearly another 40 years before both sayings were made official mottoes of Rotary. "Service, Not Self" took on its current form of "Service Above Self" at the 1950 Rotary International Convention, while "He Profits Most Who Serves Best" remained in its original form. In 1989, the Council on Legislation adopted "Service Above Self" as the primary tenet of Rotary, and later, in 2004, "He Profits Most Who Serves Best" was changed to read "They Profit Most Who Serve Best." The saying's final and current adaptation of "One Profits Most Who Serves Best" was made again by the Council of Legislation in 2010.

In its essence, "Service Above Self" means that efforts to improve the well-being of others is a fundamental priority. It means serving others is more important than serving yourself. Sometimes it requires you to subjugate your own activities or personal comfort in order to make others' lives better, without expectation of reward or praise.

Of course, if you know anything about human nature, you know there always must be something for the giver. There must be an answer to the question "What's in it for ME?" If you recall from Chapter 4, "Will it Build GOODWILL and BETTER Friendships," we discussed the nature and significance of altruism. Certainly, there is an element of this at work here.

There is a scientific basis explaining why people are motivated to help based on the merit of the help alone. James Fowler, professor of medical genetics and political science at the University of California, San Diego has conducted studies examining altruism and found that a single act of kindness can generate additional such acts. He termed it "upstream reciprocity," meaning the domino effect of positive feelings coming from kind acts. Another study, this time from Harvard Business School in 2010, sampled input from people in 136 countries. The study found that those people who consider themselves altruistic—whether through charitable donations or good works—tend to be happiest overall.

So, in the case of "Service Above Self," the answer to "What's In for ME?" is that sense of satisfaction that you have been able to help—that you made a difference in someone's life—maybe without them even knowing who provided the help. That is the very spirit of the service that Sheldon, Collins, Pinkham, Harris and so many others have embraced.

Today, the motto "Service Above Self" is synonymous with Rotary because it represents the core nature of Rotarians' volunteerism. While Rotary, as an organization, has received much recognition for the combined efforts of its members to effect positive change—both great and small—individual

Rotarians rarely receive public acclaim. When Rotarians act in keeping with the motto, they are the embodiment of the ideal of "Servant Leadership." By serving others, unselfishly and from the heart, Rotarians better their own communities, and have a global impact.

The late George Kiyoshi Togasaki (Rotary Club of Tokyo), Rotary International President from 1968-1969, summed it up quite nicely in a quote that appeared in Rotarian Magazine in 1968:

> *"We speak of Rotary as a force or movement...conjuring up visions of a great, faceless organization of nameless persons. However, Rotary is an association of individuals from many nations and many walks of life, speaking many languages and embracing many faiths—but united in the common goal of offering service to mankind above self."*

In the next section, we'll meet someone who has taken the ideal of "Service Above Self" to heart, acting because she felt she had to, in spite of great inconvenience—and even risk,—to herself. As a result, she has touched thousands of lives, improved the welfare of hundreds, and left an incredible legacy.

"HOW CAN I HELP?"

September 11, 2001 is a day no one alive then will ever forget. While we certainly all remember where we were when the World Trade Center buildings collapsed and terrorist-manned planes hit the Pentagon and a field in Pennsylvania, it was the day after that spurred Rotarian Fary Moini (La Jolla Golden Triangle Rotary Club, CA) to embark on a personal mission to help refugees and others in what was considered by many to be the "enemy camp."

September 12, 2001, Fary was watching TV when she caught a news piece showing an Afghan mother and her young daughter, running through the rubble. A reporter stopped them and began asking some questions. The mother was speaking Farsi Dari, and, although a slightly different dialect than Fary's native Iranian language, Fary was able to make out enough to understand that the woman's husband had been killed by the Taliban and she and her daughter were frantically trying to make it to Pakistan. They were frightened, they were hungry, and they were desperate. It was at that moment, Fary says, that she knew she *had* to do something, although she had no idea what or how. She was so strongly compelled to go that she felt if she didn't do it, her life would be "meaningless."

This was not the life to which Fary was accustomed. While she was born and raised in Iran, she came to the United States—San Diego, specifically—in November, 1983. Her family encouraged her to study nursing, and she eventually became a cardiology nurse, ultimately working in hospitals as far away as Dubai and Tehran. In the United States, she had an independent life, running her own businesses and making friends and new connections. That included joining Rotary.

Rotary is where she turned first when she wanted to help the refugees in Peshawar, Pakistan. Steve Brown, Fary's self-declared "mentor," was a charter member of her club and had been active with projects in Africa. He was the first she confided in about her plans. When she explained that she was able to speak Farsi and had nursing skills, he helped get her in touch with Rotarian Zamurad Shah from Uni-Town Rotary Club in Peshawar Pakistan.

Four months later, she found herself in the first of many refugee camps she would ultimately experience as a Rotary volunteer, working as an OB/GYN nurse. She explained how deplorable the conditions were in the camp when she arrived: "They didn't have a sewer system, they didn't have hot water, they didn't have baby clothes, they didn't have clothes or bed sheets, nothing." Doctors and nurses had to use food-handler gloves for deliveries and there were no adequate medications or medical equipment. Fary often stayed at the clinic with the Afghan medical staff, who were frequently refugees themselves, because there was no other place for her.

She frequently despaired at the conditions, but that despair was the catalyst for determination. She begged her Rotary club for any assistance they could offer: she asked for $600 for a generator, and the Club responded, providing her with nearly $7,000 out of members' own pockets! With that, she was able to help the clinic by building a sewer system and kitchen, buy and install a water heater, two delivery tables and more.

Upon her return, Fary was inspired to do more. She began to talk about building a school in Afghanistan for the refugee children. Again, with Fary's willpower and the help of Rotarians Steve Brown, Jan Percival and Rick Clark and others, $90,000 was raised. By 2002, they broke ground and by 2004, the Rotary Jalalabad School was open. Initially, the school consisted of a tent housing 400 students—200 boys and 200 girls. Since then, the school has grown to over 6,000 students, with computer labs, a community hall and more. The school is unique in another way: it's one of the few schools that provides an educational path for girls, especially for those wanting to go beyond eighth grade.

Fary's story is unique and exemplary in several ways. For one, she has built a tremendous connection with the locals built on mutual respect. When there were rumors of dissention among tribal elders about the perceived dangers of educating the young girls, Fary went to them and declared her commitment to keeping the girls safe, even if it meant closing the school's computer center. She received unanimous support of the school and the girls were allowed to continue to attend. This was an unexpected positive response from male tribal leaders in their first dealing with a female, and particularly one who did not conform to the conventions expected of her gender.

Against "traditional" advice, Fary dresses as a Westerner, without covering her face or head with a scarf. She says that she is representing who she is—an American, a woman, a Rotarian—and just as she respects the cultures of the Afghans, she expects them to respect hers. In her own words,

> *"A lot of foreigners came to that part [of Afghanistan] and they said because of the respect, the culture to their customs, we are wearing these scarves, we are wearing this–I am totally against it because I said I am there to help them, I'm there to assist them. I want them also to respect who I am and what is my culture, what is my customs. And then let's build a relationship in that foundation. And it worked, it worked beautifully."*

Even the religious differences could pose a stumbling block. The Afghan leaders are all devoutly Muslim, while Fary is decidedly not. She recounts a story where even her host family were hopeful that they could make her a "good Muslim," bringing her books and other educational materials, to which Fary responded, "Sweetheart, I'm too old for this change."

Fary has continued her universal mission of help over the years. She has travelled back to Afghanistan 25 times, and visited Pakistan twice. She has ventured to Turkey to train female Afghan doctors on using various medical equipment to assist with obstetrics and more. On April 20, 2012, Fary Moini was honored at a "Champions of Change" ceremony at the White House, recognized for her leadership of dozens of other successful initiatives to promote education for girls and young women, enhance the cause of peace and justice, and support the training of health care professionals in the region.

When asked about the basis for her success in helping in an area that has such economic, religious and cultural differences from what we in the United States are used to, Fary is quite candid. She credits her approach to addressing the refugees' needs, what they ask for, rather than just imposing her perception of a solution. As she said, "We foreigners, we have to understand them. They think differently, they sense differently. We have to respect them. Respect their culture... and then understand them and build on what they have, build on who they are." A "solution" that might work in a Western culture might not be appropriate—or even work—if they didn't "Afghanize" it. It's what Fary and her team did, and it worked.

That's the lesson to be learned here: the need for support and assistance is a universal one. Whether through natural disaster, economic or political conditions, or the daily stress of human conditions, our fellow man can require help at any time from those of us who are willing, able, and eager to provide that help.

By the very nature of asking the question, "How Can I Help?" we must be willing to wait for the answer, not presuppose the solution. A "fix" that isn't appropriate or wanted, isn't a fix at all, because it doesn't come from addressing the needs of the recipient. And, to go back to the Four-Way Test, a "fix" that is imposed on someone wouldn't be "BENEFICIAL to all concerned."

SUMMARY

- This chapter was dedicated to a discussion of the Four-Way Test in real-life application. Since previous chapters were about dissecting each individual Question, it's time now to look at the Test as a whole.

- One interesting aspect of looking at the individual Questions was an experiment I did, asking Rotarians through social media and my newsletter "Which of the Questions in the Four-Way Test is most important, and why?" The answers were very well thought-out and each respondent had a great argument for why they felt their answer was justified.

- As a result of a social media query, I began receiving submissions from Clubs across the globe, reporting that they had taken the question to their membership and sharing results. I've now issued a global "Most Important Question Challenge..." and look forward to getting more feedback and sharing it broadly.

- The reality is that the Four-Way Test must be used in its entirety. You cannot merely choose to adhere to one of the questions or even a few. If any single question in the Test doesn't pass, then the entire Test fails, much like an old-fashioned truth table.

- Another hallmark motto of Rotary is "Service Above Self." We looked at the history of this phrase and other related sayings over Rotary's history.

- The true definition of "Service above Self" is showing acts of kindness to others, including total strangers, knowing you may never be recognized. You must push yourself beyond normal boundaries for the betterment of others, making yourself uncomfortable in order to make others more comfortable. It may be that the only reward is the satisfaction in the effort and results you achieve.

♦ Our case study involved Fary Moini, whose efforts to help refugees in Afghanistan and Pakistan fleeing from their native countries after 9/11, crossed not only borders, but also religions, cultures, genders and beliefs. Iranian-born Fary's efforts first as a nurse, and then later as the point-person inspired to build a major community school, showed that compassion and the desire to help others in need transcends all perceived differences. More importantly, Fary and her team saw great acceptance and success in their efforts because they approached their aid from the perspective of the needs of the Afghan people themselves. Rather than assume they knew the "solution," they respected the culture and concerns of their recipients and provided support that was "BENEFICIAL to all concerned."

YOUR TURN

In this chapter, we considered the Four-Way Test in its entirety, applying it to life issues. We also examined the motto of "Service Above Self" and "One Profits Most Who Serves Best." Again, you may want to just do these exercises yourself, or perhaps you'd like to share them with your club or other group. These questions are meant to be points of discussion, and may raise topics of your own.

- ❑ What do those phrases mean to you, personally and/or professionally? Can you identify some instances where you have had to make difficult decisions and used the Four-Way Test as a yardstick?

- ❑ What does "Servant Leadership" mean to you? What is your own leadership or management style, even if it is only within a family unit? We are all managing and leading in one form or another.

- ❑ Have you personally taken on any projects where the motive is merely the service itself on its own merits? Perhaps you'd like to share the circumstances, results and how you felt.

- ❑ What do you think about the idea of "Pay it Forward?" Have you personally done this? How could you "Pay it Forward" in your community, Club or even the world at large?

- ❑ If you haven't been able to "give" more of yourself, ask yourself why. Is it time? Do the projects at hand not fit your goals and objectives? Everyone has a reason for why they aren't able to do more for others; if service is important, then it's worth finding your constraints and seeing what you can do about it.

❑ Mega-author and inspirational speaker Brian Tracy in his book "No Excuses" says: "What kind of world would this be if everyone in it was just like me?" What if everyone had the ability to learn about the Four-Way Test and "Service Above Self" at an earlier age? How do you think the world would be different? What could we accomplish?

❑ What can you do TODAY to perform an act of "Service Above Self?" The Boy Scouts have a practice of taking a special coin and moving it to their right pocket after they have done a good deed. Can you adapt this "Do a Good Turn Daily" practice in your own life?

CHAPTER 9

THE FOUR-WAY TEST AND THE GOLDEN RULE

"The Rotary way is the Confucius way. The Rotary way is to light a candle. I light you, you light one, 1.2 million Rotarians light one. Together, we light up the world"

— *Rotary International President Gary C.K. Huang*

In the previous chapter, we discussed how the Four-Way Test can be applied in life—both in everyday life, and in extraordinary situations. This chapter, however, takes a different twist and asks the question, "How *applicable* is the Four-Way Test?" Is it something that can be universally applied, or does it only work for those who have a particular philosophy or religious/spiritual leaning? Let's explore that together!

ROTARY AND "RELIGION"

Along with politics and money, religion is one of those big topics that can quickly lead to heated and opinionated discussions. It is often avoided altogether, in an attempt to stay clear of these heated contests. And, religion is further tricky because the ideas of what constitute a religion are completely subjective. In the same way we talked about "moral relativism" in Chapter 6, we could here talk about "religious relativism" because there isn't one "right or wrong" belief. Oh, sure, there are certainly individuals and groups that would argue that their perspective is the only correct one, and the rest of us are going to hell...but what do you do if your particular belief system doesn't include a "hell" in its doctrine?

Religion, and what people believe, is certainly an interesting topic. People can be very passionate about what they do—or don't—believe in and why. One interesting example of this is Thomas Jefferson, the third President of the United States. He was a deeply spiritual man, but one who couldn't accept the concept of a religious establishment. Personally, he did not believe in Christ as a deity. Because of his belief and appreciation that "religion" is an individually personal matter and not something to be "imposed upon" others, —and certainly *not* by governments, —he proposed the original concept of "Separation of Church and State." In an 1802 letter to the Danbury Baptist Association, Jefferson wrote:

> *"Believing with you that religion is a matter which lies solely between Man & his God, that he owes account to none other for his faith or his worship, that the legitimate powers of government reach actions only, & not opinions, I contemplate with sovereign reverence that act of the whole American people which declared that their legislature should 'make no law respecting an establishment of religion, or prohibiting the free exercise thereof,' thus building a wall of separation between Church & State."*

In other words, the government was not to dictate religious beliefs or practices, although it was to allow for the freedom of individual religious expression. The government was supposed to remain at arms-length in matters of religion, and leave that up to the people.

There is also this practical difference between "religion" and "spirituality." One definition of "religion" is "a cause, principle, or system of beliefs held to with ardor and faith." It also refers to the "practice" of this belief, whether personal or institutionalized. What President Jefferson believed was, "personal, yes. Institutional, no."

Examining the idea of being "spiritual," however, has us considering the definition that it's "of or relating to sacred matters," or "ecclesiastical rather than lay or temporal." Further in the definition of spiritual, we get this: "of or relating to supernatural beings or phenomena." Spiritual, by its definition seems to be a much more internalized concept, — note it says nothing about *practice,* — whereas "religion" relates to actions, not just beliefs.

So, how does this relate to Rotary and the Four-Way Test? You might be surprised at how "religion" figured into its creation and adoption, and what that means for us now.

"Is it the 'Biblical' TRUTH?"

In Chapter 1, we introduced the Four-Way Test and talked a bit about its author, Herbert J. Taylor. While we certainly celebrate him for penning this important ethical yardstick, Herbert himself really would take little credit for it. Taylor was a deeply devout Christian, raised as a Methodist. He was involved in his own church and with several other Christian organizations, including co-founding the Christian Workers Federation, and participating on the boards of such groups as Youth for Christ, Young Life, the Fuller Seminary, Pioneer Girls and the Greater Chicago Billy Graham Crusades.

It was Taylor's personal belief that the Four-Way Test actually came to him through prayer. He felt that "God has a plan for all of us," and that this belief is what led to the positive accomplishments in his life, including his involvement in Rotary and the drafting of the Four-Way Test. As a solution to the challenges his company, Club Aluminum, was facing, Taylor explained that he needed to "set policies for the company that would reflect the high ethics and morals God would want in any business." Thus, the Four-Way Test was born.

His concern over the appropriateness of the Four-Way Test as a yardstick for ethical behavior for his employees led Taylor to share it with four managers at Club Aluminum. These managers were of different religions: an Orthodox Jew, a Roman Catholic, a Presbyterian and a Christian Scientist. Taylor wanted to be sure that the creed he was promoting would not conflict with any of their individual or collective religious beliefs, in the hopes of, therefore, being consistent with the beliefs of all his employees.

"Religious" practices?

As we learned in Chapter 1, the Four-Way Test was not originally an exclusively-Rotarian creed, and while it was introduced to Rotary by Taylor in 1938, in wasn't actually adopted by Rotary until 1952. In spite of the "Godly" origins Herbert Taylor attributes, there is nothing overtly religious about the Four-Way Test.

If you recall from our discussion earlier in this chapter, "religion" speaks more to the practice of the belief than the belief itself.

So, to relate this to the Four-Way Test, we can say that the four questions are philosophical—they are a set of "beliefs," the *spirit,* that we must apply. What we apply them to *is the practice* of that belief: "of the things we think, say and do..."

In fact, there are other elements of "religious" practice that take place at many Rotary Clubs. One example of this is the invocation or blessing of the meeting or before the meal. Depending on the Club's membership, this activity can be a decidedly religious event—it can be a formal or informal prayer. But, just as with separation of Church and State, Rotary itself does not require this as part of a standard meeting format. It is left up to the Club, and also the individuals within the Club, to participate in this practice.

Sometimes the "inspirational thought for the day" is quite religion-neutral. As the world—and organizations such as Rotary—has become more diverse, the goal has been to achieve a balance between recognizing and honoring traditional forms of expression while not excluding other forms of religion or spirituality. For example, one variant of the traditional Christian prayer conclusion ("In Jesus' name we pray") is "In our God we pray..." to recognize that we may have a personal version of a deity in whom we believe, but that another person may hold a different belief.

And, again, this is completely consistent with the spirit of the Four-Way Test. As Taylor recognized, when he asked his four managers to review the Test in light of their own religious beliefs, in order to work for *all* it had to be appropriate for *all.* In the next section, we'll explore another such "test" that also has broad application. It is another principle for living happy and successful lives.

THE GOLDEN RULE

Herbert Taylor was not the only person to believe in the need for, or to offer aa universal test of ethics. Nor was he by any means the first. The idea of humankind needing to adhere to some form of mutual support and protection is as old as mankind itself. Without being able to look after a family group or community, that group would leave itself open to all manner of harm and face a very real risk of dying off.

While today, we don't generally face the same degree of daily life-threatening risks by predators as our cavemen ancestors did, there is still a need for some guidance on how we manage our collective existence, whether it's within our local communities or on a national or global level. And, through the ages, across cultures and religions, mankind overall has generally agreed.

We have probably all heard of The Golden Rule. The most common reference for it is from the Bible. The King James Version states it as "Therefore all things whatsoever ye would that men should do to you, do ye even so to them: for this is the law and the prophets." (Matthew 7:12). However, a more common phrase is "Do unto others as you would have them do unto you." In SocialSmarts, we simplified the phrase so that even the youngest kids could memorize it and understand it: "Treat others the way you want them to treat you."

The idea of a Golden Rule is quite universal; it transcends religion, culture and belief. Consider some of these "rules" and how similar they are to the Biblical version:

> *"Do not do to others that which would anger you if others did to you."*—Socrates, c. 450 BC

"May I do to others as I would that they should do unto me."—Plato c. 400 BC

"We should behave to others as we wish others to behave to us."—Aristotle, c. 300 BC

"Hurt not others in ways that you yourself would find hurtful."—Buddha c. 4 BC

"None of you will have faith until one desires for his brother what he desires for himself."—Muhammed c. 600 AD

"The heart of the person before you is a mirror. See there your own form." —Munetada Kurozumi (1780-1850), founder of the Shinto religion

"Regard your neighbor's gain as your gain, and your neighbor's loss as your own loss."—Taoist Scripture

"This is the sum of duty: do not unto others which would cause you pain if done to you."—Hindu writings Mahabharata

The revered Chinese teacher and philosopher, Confucius, himself made the Golden Rule the indisputable centerpiece of his philosophy on life. Confucius believed that his version of the rule, *Kung-shu*, came fully-developed from the very lips and writings of the "Morality Giver" and in seemingly universal form. It makes for an interesting foreshadowing of Herbert Taylor's own beliefs about the Four-Way Test.

But, apparently, the universal rule did not need a religious seed from which to spring forth. Even Immanuel Kant (1724-1804), the German philosopher known for his "enlightened" thinking of the human condition, morality, and frequently atheistic leanings, has his version of the "rule:"

> *"Act as if the maxim of thy action were to become by thy will a universal law of nature."*

Kant was actually one of the earliest supporters of the idea that perpetual peace could be brought about through universal democracy and international cooperation. Certainly, this was a novel concept at a tumultuous time in the world's history, when wars, invasions and colonization were continuous.

The Golden Rule is easier to follow when it's used within the comfort of your own local family or community group, in other words, to others that are *relevant* to you. But when you begin to examine and apply it in broader terms, across cultures, the idea behind a universal law becomes revolutionary. "Treat *all* others" that way? Can that even be done?

Not only can it be done—it must. While you could argue that not everyone is going to adhere to the concept,—much less the *practice*,—of the rule, the reality is that it's the only way to overcome our collective challenges. Without some form of the Golden Rule in place, we don't have a society or community—we have anarchy.

Regardless of the version you use, the "rule" is about reciprocity. And, that is the essence of the Four-Way Test—in all you think, say and do, be mindful of the impression and impact on the other person or persons in the equation. Treat them with the same consideration you yourself expect. There's nothing difficult about that concept, although there can certainly be challenges when you apply it. There will be times where others are not treating you justly or kindly; there may be people actively trying to slander or hurt you in some way. But the Rule doesn't say "treat others the way they treat you," but rather treat them the way you *want* to be treated. Taoism puts that quite succinctly when it states:

> *"To those who are good to me, I am good; to those who are not good to me, I am also good. Thus all get to be good."*

So, if the Golden Rule and the Four-Way Test are so similar, why have a separate "pledge" at all? Why not just adopt and use the Golden Rule? Well, as a matter of fact, this was the direction Rotary was headed, because the Golden Rule is a guide for ethical conduct—the very concept that Rotary espoused.

Yet, in 1935, Paul Harris had concerns about broad adoption of the Golden Rule because of its close association to mainstream Christian religious practice. Although, as we've seen, there are plenty of "non-religious" versions. Paul Harris wrote in his book *This Rotarian Age,*

> *"The retention of the Golden Rule as a summation of the hopes and ambitions of Rotary has recently met with serious opposition from different quarters. It is not that any appreciable number lack faith in the Golden Rule as a guide in the affairs of men. The objection most frequently heard is that it has so long been identified with religious movements that its adoption by Rotary affords reasonable grounds for the assumption by the uninitiated that Rotary is in fact a religion."*

So, the solution to this conundrum was the Four-Way Test, which is really a more detailed "how to" of the Golden Rule. But it, like Rotary, makes no reference or recommendation of any religious practice or belief. It relies instead on the universal ethical imperative for treating our fellow man with dignity and decency.

NON-RELIGIOUS DOES NOT MEAN ANTI-RELIGIOUS

While Rotary itself has no ties to any specific religions or religious practices, that does not mean the organization is anti-religion. In fact, there is a deep-seated respect for the belief systems and practices of all its members. While Rotary was formed at a time where most of its members were from American mainstream Christian churches, no one was excluded on the basis of religion. And today, you'll find members from all belief systems, including those who have no belief system, equally supported, equally valued.

Even the Rotary motto of "Service above Self," has at its core the ideal of serving others first which is common to many of the world's religions. K.R. Ravindran, Rotary International President (2015-16), made reference to the link between the motto and religions when he spoke at the 2015 Parliament of World Religions in Salt Lake City, Utah:

> "Service gives people a way to come together and a reason to work together for the common good, regardless of their differences. Charity and serving those with the greatest needs are ideas common to every religion, which is what Rotary is all about."

So, the fundamentals and practices of Rotary are quite well-aligned and consistent with virtually all the mainstream religions, even though it makes no religious prescription of its own. The basic rules for decent conduct are the same: be kind to one another, treat others fairly and act with love and respect. That's the beauty of a Universal Truth: it's with us all the time and applies no matter what we are doing and who we are doing it with.

PROMOTING UNDERSTANDING ACROSS RELIGIONS

As we discussed earlier, the topic of religion can be a very controversial one, one that is sure to spark debate and, frequently, dissension. People tend to take their spiritual beliefs and practices very seriously. Often dialog and questioning of others' viewpoints can be interpreted as personal attacks.

As we know, Rotary is religion-neutral in principle and practice. However, individual members and religious groups can still find themselves at odds, regardless of their good intentions. It can require a strong and steady effort to bridge those differences of opinion and affiliation. Let's look at one man's lifelong efforts to bring understanding and acceptance among different religious groups.

Sir Sigmund Sternberg was born in Hungary in 1921, the only son of an Orthodox Jewish family. Even growing up, he was aware of the tensions between religions. He attended a Jewish gymnasium school, but later attended a commercial college. One day, he got into a fight with a Catholic student who accused Steinberg of killing Jesus. His family sent him to England as the political tension in Europe increased. He wanted to enlist in the British military, but was disqualified because he was considered a "friendly enemy alien." He got involved in civil defense instead, working in the scrap metal industry, where he ultimately made his fortune after the war. He was naturalized as a British citizen in 1947.

Sternberg became increasingly involved in business, philanthropy and community service, founding his own Sternberg Charitable Foundation in 1968. He was deeply involved in service organizations such as Rotary (Rotary Club of London) and the Movement for Reform Judaism, where he served as President. He had a keen interest in interfaith relations and joined the International Council of Christians and Jews in 1979. The Council was originally formed in 1946 as a result of the Jewish Holocaust, in order to create dialog and understanding between Christians and Jews.

Sternberg worked tirelessly to buffer Judeo-Christian relations and promote social justice, orchestrating a first-ever visit by a Pope, John Paul II, to the Tempeo Maggiore, Rome's Great Synagogue, in 1986. This facilitated dialog between the Vatican and Israel. He also helped form the Three Faiths Forum, which sought to encourage mutual understanding between Judaism, Christianity and Islam.

One notable event, for which Sternberg is widely recognized, was his effort to affect the removal of a Carmelite convent that had been built in the 1980s along the site of the concentration camp, Auschwitz, in Poland. While the nuns had the noble intention of praying and honoring the victims of the camp, many felt that their presence was inappropriate where nearly 2 million Jews had lost their lives. It became a hotly contested issue. Sternberg became involved in the Geneva Declaration, and helped ease the tensions that had been increasing between Jews and Christians globally over this issue. Sternberg helped negotiate a plan with Poland's Cardinal Josef Glemp, and the convent was moved in 1993.

Sternberg received many honors during and after his lifetime from many sources for his work. He was knighted by Queen Elizabeth II in 1976. Pope John Paul II recognized him as Knight Commander of the Pontifical and Equestrian Order of St. Gregory the Great. In 1998, in recognition of his "advanced public understanding of God and spirituality," he was awarded the Templeton Prize. For both the Templeton Prize and the Knight Commander citation, he was only the second Jew to be ever so honored.

In November 2005, Sternberg was promoted to the highest rank within the Royal Order of Francis I to the grade of Knight Grand Cross (GCFO). The Royal Order was initially established in 1829 as an award of merit for distinction in public service, science, the arts, agriculture, industry and commerce. Sir Sternberg received his promotion for his services to charity and inter-religious understanding. In 2008, the Bishop of London bestowed Sternberg with the St. Mellitus Medal, recognizing his continued efforts towards positive interfaith relations.

Sir Sigmund died in 2016, but left a legacy of working to improve communications and understanding between religions. He was once quoted to say: "Confrontations in interfaith relations never succeed. The only way forward is through respectful dialogue." It seems Sir Sigmund understood the intent and the practice of the Four-Way Test. His work was devoted to "building GOODWILL and better FRIENDSHIPS." His listing among the 100 Great Rotarians is well-deserved.

SUMMARY

In this Chapter, we examined two very similar "general" creeds for conduct, integrity and ethics to determine how valid they are across varying cultures and belief systems. Both, when applied consistently, can, as past RI President C.K. Huang said, "light up the world."

- An important criterion for a general rule of conduct is how applicable it is. As we learned, when Herbert Taylor first proposed the Four-Way Test as a yardstick for measuring the actions and intent of his employees at Club Aluminum, he asked four managers of differing religions to weigh in on whether his "test" violated any of their beliefs or practices. The managers found no problems in his proposed questions.

- Similarly, the Golden Rule—frequently stated as "Treat others the way you want them to treat you,"—is a test that also has broad applicability. We saw many different variants of this "rule," from a multitude of religions and non-religious beliefs, all which contained some form of "looking out and caring for another."

- Although the Four-Way Test and the Golden Rule are highly similar in intent, the Golden Rule was not adopted by Rotary because of its strong identification with religion. Since Rotary makes no prescription for religious practices, the Four-Way Test (in spite of Taylor's self-reported "divine" inspiration for the Test) was deemed a better fit.

- Because of its global nature, Rotary welcomes members from all walks of life, religions and cultures. Rotary International itself has no specific affiliation with any religion, nor does it call for any religious practices as part of its requirements for Clubs or individual members. Any religious observances, such as prayer to start the meetings, is a choice made at the club or individual member level. Many clubs, seeking to be more inclusive, have opted for more general rituals instead of a prayer or invocation. "Inspirational Moments," or similar segments are becoming more common as Clubs strive to respect others' beliefs or practices.

+ Speaking of religion, this chapter also drilled down into the differences between "religion" and "spirituality," which frequently are used interchangeably, but aren't exactly the same. Religion generally refers to a practice or an organized group which believes and practices a specific way, whereas "spirituality" is a more internalized concept meaning "relating to sacred matters."

+ While it is easy to apply both the Four-Way Test and the Golden Rule in situations where you have a personal or otherwise positive relationship with the other party, to be true to the spirit of both creeds, they must apply at all times, in all cases, regardless of whether the other person is treating you fairly or positively.

+ Both the Golden Rule and the Four-Way Test are rules of reciprocity. The goal of any interaction using both "tests" is to leave a positive impression on the other party involved.

+ The story of Sir Sigmund Steinberg is one that illustrates the power of mutual respect when trying to bridge cultures or religions. Sir Sigmund dedicated his life to philanthropic, civic and service efforts, becoming notable for tirelessly working to bring better understanding and communication among differing religious groups.

YOUR TURN

There are any number of scenarios and opportunities for evaluating and practicing the concepts we discussed in this chapter. Here are a few that may not be so obvious, but might be a great start for thought or dialog.

❑ In today's day and age, religion can be such a tricky subject. Do you personally avoid sharing your beliefs or practices with another out of concern you may offend? It might be something so simple as wishing someone "Merry Christmas" or even "Happy Thanksgiving" (said by some to be offensive to Native Americans). How do your own beliefs affect what you do/say with others?

❑ What sort of "inspirational" practices does your Club support? If your Club offers an "inspirational moment" or "thought for the day," is the expectation that this sharing is to be strictly non-religious or is there room for individual expression? How do you members feel about the types of practices you participate in?

❑ When you are faced with a difficult person or situation, do you stop to consider your thoughts/actions in light of either the Golden Rule or the Four-Way Test before you proceed? For some, this type of analysis is or has become instinctive. Most of us probably need more practice in this area. Where do you think you fall on this continuum? Where would you like to be?

- ❏ Do you believe that individuals can be spiritual but not religious? How about the reverse?

- ❏ Regardless of your faith, religious practices or beliefs, how tolerant and open are you of others' practices? What, if anything, could you do to improve communication and understanding between differing ideologies?

- ❏ One woman's response to the question of her religious belief was: "Rotary is my religion!" What do you think she meant by that? What is your feeling on "Rotary=religion?"

CHAPTER 10

IN CONCLUSION

"We make a living from what we get; we
make a life from what we give."

— *Winston Churchill (honorary Rotarian)*

In the preceding chapters, we took a comprehensive journey, examining each question in the Four-Way Test. We explored the meaning and implications of each question. We met individuals who have lived the virtues embodied in them. As we reach the end of the book, I think it's fitting to recap the immense character content represented by the Four-Way Test. These brief 24 words contain a wealth of wisdom, and can literally be the key to greater personal and professional success. The list of character foundations we find captured in the Four-Way Test include:

- Honesty and Integrity
- Fairness and Equality
- Empathy, Kindness, Caring and Respect
- Consideration, Cooperation and Fairness

As we looked further into the components of Integrity, we also considered:

- Responsibility
- Reliability
- Courage
- Loyalty

Recall, too, that we considered the virtues of Tolerance and Acceptance. We explored how they differ, and why one is more productive and powerful than the other.

For those of you keeping track, that's FIFTEEN crucial character components all contained in those 24 little words! And the best part about it is that the precepts offered in the Four-Way Test are generally applicable and appropriate, no matter your culture, religious beliefs, gender or life-experience. Just like the Golden Rule—and its many variations—it proposes a way of thinking and acting that will put you in a better position to be happier and more successful in your personal and professional life

IT'S THE RIGHT THING TO DO

Rotary has a number of different beliefs and mottos that are all designed to work together to provide definition and guidance for who we are and how we are to conduct ourselves. Specifically, what we have explored in this book directly supports the Second Object of Rotary, which reads:

> *SECOND: High ethical standards in business and professions; the recognition of the worthiness of all useful occupations; and the dignifying of each Rotarian's occupation as an opportunity to serve society;*

Of course, as we have recognized, we can expand the ideals of all the mottos and creeds in Rotary to include personal attitude and conduct, in addition to our professional lives. We don't stop being Rotarians the moment we leave the office

There are, certainly, many strategic reasons why thinking and behaving with positive social skills and character is beneficial. As we teach in SocialSmarts™, you are likely to "get more of what you want, more easily—and less of what you don't want." But, living this way comes down to a more basic truth: It's the right thing to do. Stay within the rules, keep within the lines, and life does become a little simpler. You may not be able to affect the behavior of others or control life's external circumstances, but you do have the ability to manage your own behavior, and your own responses. You will know that you've done the best you could do. That's really all anyone can expect.

LIFE-CHANGING IMPACTS

I would like to leave you with one final story. If you recall from Chapter 8, I wrote about Fary Moini and her efforts in Afghanistan. During my nearly 2-hour interview with her, she mentioned a short parable that has always resonated strongly with me. In fact, I use it in several of my presentations and assemblies for students and adults. Perhaps you are already familiar with it, but I never tire hearing it. I hope you find it as inspiring as I do. It's originally from "The Star Thrower," published in 1978 by Loren Eisley, an American philosopher.

The Story of the Starfish

Once upon a time, there was an old man who had a habit of walking on the beach every morning before he began his work. This one particular morning, he was walking along the shore after a big storm had passed and found the beach littered with starfish as far as the eye could see, stretching in both directions.

Off in the distance, the old man noticed a small boy on the sand. The old man noticed that as the boy walked along the beach, he paused every so often, bending down to pick up an object and throw it into the sea. The boy continued along, coming closer but continuing his bending and tossing. Finally, the boy was close enough that the old man called out, "Good morning! May I ask what it is that you are doing?"

The young boy paused, looked up, and answered, "Throwing starfish into the ocean. The storm washed them onto the beach and they can't return to the ocean by themselves," The boy explained, "When the sun gets high and hot, they'll die, so I'm throwing them back into the water."

The old man replied, "But there must be tens of thousands of starfish on this beach. Son, I'm afraid you won't really be able to make much of a difference."

The boy bent down, picked up yet another starfish and threw it as far as he could into the ocean. Then he turned, looked the old man in the eyes, smiled and said, "I made a difference to that one!"

—*—

I believe that is the spirit of the Four-Way Test. To stop and think, to evaluate what we are about to say and do before we take action, and consider the effects of those words and deeds on others. As Rotarians, we have the power to positively impact many people and circumstances, as we've seen throughout the organization's history. But we also have the ability to do great harm and hurt, if we forget our roots and charter.

Like our character and our social skills, the Four-Way Test is the guidepost for who we are and how we conduct ourselves, no matter what else we are doing. Unlike our meetings, there's no "makeup" for life. Let's be the very best we can be, each and every day, with all with whom we concern ourselves. That, my friends, is how we succeed in "Making a Difference" (Rotary Theme, 2017-2018)

Thank you for being on this journey with me.

SELECTED BIBLIOGRAPHY & OTHER RESOUCES

More About Famous Rotarians

http://www.rotaractorwiki.org/wiki/Famous_Rotarians

http://www.charlotterotary.org/40ofamousrotarians.html

http://www.rotaractorwiki.org/images/b/b9/100RotaryQuotes.pdf

Herbert J. Taylor

http://anbhf.org/laureates/herbert-taylor/

https://en.wikipedia.org/wiki/Herbert_J._Taylor

Woodrow Wilson

https://en.wikipedia.org/wiki/Woodrow_Wilson

http://millercenter.org/president/biography/wilson-life-in-brief);

Frank Borman

http://www.nationalaviation.org/our-enshrinees/borman-frank/

https://en.wikipedia.org/wiki/Eastern_Air_Lines_Flight_401

Sir Edmund Hilary

http://www.siredmundhillary.com/trust.htm

http://www.biography.com/people/edmund-hillary-9339111#death-and-legacy

Dr. Charles H Mayo

http://www.encyclopedia.com/history/encyclopedias-almanacs-transcripts-and-maps/william-j-and-charles-h-mayo

https://en.wikipedia.org/wiki/Mayo_Clinic

W. Horace Carter and Willard G. Cole

https://books.google.com/books?id=6UMOAQAAMAAJ&q=
horace+cole+ Pulitzer+prize&dq=horace+cole+Pulitzer+ prize&hl=en&sa=
X&ved=oahUKEwiQsca67OfSAhVK22MKHYMlDqoQ6AEIKTAB

https://en.wikipedia.org/wiki/W._Horace_Carter

Duke Kahanamoko

https://www.nytimes.com/2014/08/23/upshot/duke-of-hawaii-a-
swimmer-and-surfer-who-straddled-two-cultures.html?_r=o

https://en.wikipedia.org/wiki/Duke_Kahanamoku

http://www.encyclopedia.com/people/sports-and-games/
sports-biographies/duke-kahanamoku

Fary Moini

http://www.lajollalight.com/sdljl-fary-moini-joins-the-rotary-
to-help-around-the-2010dec15-story.html

http://www.sandiegouniontribune.com/lifestyle/making-a-
difference/sd-me-difference-rotary-20170419-story.html

Thomas Jefferson

https://www.usconstitution.net/jeffwall.html

Sir Sigmund Steinberg

https://www.ft.com/content/6572fo44-9c41-11e6-a6e4-8b8e77ddo83a

https://www.ft.com/content/6572fo44-9c41-11e6-a6e4-8b8e77ddo83a

OTHER RESOURCES

"It's Not Who You Know, It's How You Treat Them: Five SocialSmarts Secrets Today's Business Leaders Need to Stand Out and be Successful," by Corinne Gregory

http://corinnegregory.com/products-3/

The Official Site for Rotary International

https://www.rotary.org

Rotary International Leader, Corporate CEO, Challenges All to Respect Religious Traditions

https://www.forbes.com/sites/devinthorpe/2015/10/13/rotary-international-leader-corporate-ceo-challenges-all-to-respect-religious-traditions/#206967be5fc8

100 Great Rotarians

http://midjerseycaperotary.org/stories/100-famous-rotarians/

4-Way Test Association

http://www.4waytest.org/

My Purpose Driven Life: – Day 19 – Part 5: The Four Way Test

http://disciplewalk.com/ambidextrous/2013/04/06/my-purpose-driven-life-day-19-part-5-the-four-way-test/

50 Things Every Rotarian Should Know About Rotary

http://beachrotary.org/is-rotary-for-you/learn-about-rotary/50-things-every-rotarian-should-know-about-rotary/

"'Pay It Forward' Pays Off;" UC San Diego News Center, March 2010.

http://ucsdnews.ucsd.edu/archive/newsrel/soc/03-08ExperimentalFindings.asp

The PoliteChild and the SocialSmarts™ curriculum

https://www.socialsmarts.com

To Contact Corinne for More Information or Speaker Requests
corinne@corinnegregory.com • 206-271-8080

The Social Smarts Rotary Donation Program

There is a unique opportunity for Rotary Clubs to take an active role in helping schools—both public and private — make substantial changes to their students', staff, and families' lives. A Rotary Club can sponsor a SocialSmarts program in their local school, at a substantial discount over what the school would normally pay for the program. In brief, here is what it looks like when a Club sponsors a school:

- SocialSmarts waives all license fees (normally $6/student/year)
- Rotary helps underwrite materials costs and possibly training costs (as little as $2/student US)
- Schools must have some active investment and requirements for tracking/reporting results
- Rotary Clubs may add a logo or other brand to the SocialSmarts materials as visible reminder of their support

The sponsorship model has been used successfully in a number of schools across the US. The program is also appropriate for international use and Parent's Guides have been translated into Spanish.

For more information about the Rotary Sponsorship program, how it works and its results, please send me an email to corinneg@socialsmarts.com with the subject "Rotary Donation Request"

Other Rotary-underwriting opportunities exist as well. Speaking engagements, training, school and community assemblies have all been sponsored or underwritten by Rotary Clubs both in the US and abroad.

Made in the USA
Middletown, DE
15 April 2018